HAWAI'I'S BEST QUICK & EASY RECIPES

Other books by

Jean Watanabe Hee:

6 in. x 9 in • softcover, concealed wire-o bound • Retail: $14.95

Best of the Best Hawai'i Recipes

176 pp

ISBN-10: 1-56647-842-1
ISBN-13: 978-1-56647-842-7

Hawai'i's Best Salads, Sides & Soups

160 pp

ISBN-10: 1-56647-781-6
ISBN-13: 978-1-56647-781-9

Hawai'i's Best Pūpū & Potluck

152 pp

ISBN-10: 1-56647-654-2
ISBN-13: 978-1-56647-654-6

Hawai'i's Best Local Dishes

170 pages

ISBN-10: 1-56647-570-8
ISBN-13: 978-1-56647-570-9

Hawai'i's Best Local Desserts

128 pp

ISBN-10: 1-56647-518-X
ISBN-13: 978-1-56647-518-1

Hawai'i's Best Mochi Recipes

128 pp

ISBN-10: 1-56647-336-5
ISBN-13: 978-1-56647-336-1

4.25 in. x 6 in. • hardcover • Retail: $7.95

Tastes & Flavors of Mochi

64 pp

ISBN-10: 1-56647-754-9
ISBN-13: 978-1-56647-754-3

Little Hawaiian Cookbook

80 pp

ISBN-10: 1-56647-793-X
ISBN-13: 978-1-56647-793-2

To order please visit our website:
www.mutualpublishing.com
or email us at *info@mutualpublishing.com*

HAWAI'I'S BEST QUICK & EASY RECIPES

Jean Watanabe Hee

MUTUAL PUBLISHING

Library of Congress Cataloging-in-Publication Data

Hee, Jean Watanabe.
Hawaii's best quick and easy recipes / Jean Watanabe Hee.
p. cm.
Includes index.
ISBN 1-56647-901-0 (softcover : alk. paper)
1. Hawaiian cookery. 2. Quick and easy cookery. I. Title.
TX724.5.H3H4453 2009
641.59969--dc22
2009016057

ISBN-10: 1-56647-901-0
ISBN-13: 978-1-56647-901-1

Art direction by Jane Gillespie
Photography by Kaz Tanabe
Design by Courtney Young

First Printing, July 2009
Second Printing, March 2010
Third Printing, March 2012
Fourth Printing, November 2014

Mutual Publishing, LLC
1215 Center Street, Suite 210
Honolulu, Hawai'i 96816
Ph: 808-732-1709 / Fax: 808-734-4094
email: info@mutualpublishing.com
www.mutualpublishing.com

Printed in Korea

This cookbook is dedicated
in loving memory to my mother,
Asae Watanabe

and to my cousin,
Judy Kodani Takabayashi.

Table of Contents

Recipes with ↻ are *Quick & Easy*

Soups

Salads

Sides

Main Dishes

BEEF

Acknowledgments

A special thank you to my daughter, Jennifer. She has been my invaluable assistant in all ways, from helping me test recipes and giving her evaluation and recommendations, to helping me on the computer whenever I needed her expertise. I appreciate her patience and support and good humor. I'm so happy and grateful that she decided to return to work in Hawai'i and that she was able to be a part of this cookbook.

Again, I also need to thank my friends and good neighbors who helped me to gather recipes for this book. Evelyn Shiraki and Ruby Saito are two who looked out for quick and easy recipes from their own collections and from friends and shared them with me so I could test them and rewrite them for easy cooking. Merv Chun is another who would just whip out a recipe from his memory bank and dictate the ingredients to me. I would not have been able to gather such a collection of easy recipes if not for all the rest of you who willingly shared your recipes.

I also need to acknowledge my cousin, Judy Takabayashi, who made an effort to share her recipes with me. She will always be remembered.

Introduction

There have been many requests from young adults and busy working parents for a quick and easy local-style recipe cookbook. I began looking through my files, school cookbooks, church and community-produced cookbooks and asking friends, relatives and anyone who seemed interested in my cookbooks if they had any quick and easy recipes. Responses were friendly and supportive. Some popular recipes were mentioned over and over again. Some recommended recipes were considered "quick and easy" by the donors. And they were, in comparison to another similar dish. So I included them although they did have more ingredients.

Many of the recipes in this cookbook use canned goods to make them quick and easy. For example, chicken broth is a very popular base for many soups. Canned goods can be expensive but they can be bought on sale and kept in the cupboard for the time when it becomes necessary to quickly put together something to eat for your family. Do try "Alex's Quick Clam Chowder."

I tried to find good tasting dishes with a reduced number of ingredients to make it easier. So taste-testing became very important. The reduced ingredient "Guacamole" had to be acceptable and tasty, for example. The simple "Tofu Salad" is another example.

Some of my favorite dishes in this cookbook are easy to prepare, but have more ingredients. Other recipes are easy and preparation is minimal, but they require an hour or more to cook. So they are not really quick. But they are easy! The dessert section is a good example. The "No-Fail Roast Beef" is another. I also wanted to include these recipes because they are great easy recipes. So this cookbook will include "quick and easy" and "easy" recipes. "Quick and easy" recipes will be designated with a logo. I hope you will find this cookbook helpful with its easy and "quick and easy" dishes.

Pūpū

Artichoke Dip

Yield: 2 cups

1 package cream cheese (8 oz.), softened
1 jar marinated artichoke hearts (6 oz.), drained and chopped
⅓ cup sour cream
2 tablespoons green onions
1 tablespoon pimientos, chopped

Combine all ingredients and mix together.

- SUGGESTION: *Microwave Artichoke Dip in microwave for 3 to 4 minutes for a hot dip.*

Clam Dip

Yield: 1½ cups

1 can minced clams (7.5 oz.), drained (reserve clam juice)
1 package cream cheese (8 oz.), softened at room temperature
1 heaping tablespoon mayonnaise
1 teaspoon lemon juice
1 tablespoon onion, finely minced
Salt and pepper to taste
Worcestershire® sauce, to taste (optional)

Blend cream cheese, mayonnaise and enough clam juice for good dipping consistency. Add rest of ingredients. Chill. Serve with chips.

- NOTE: *For more clams, drain another can of minced clams and add to dip. This is such a great "oldie but goodie" tested recipe that goes back about 30 years ago when Jean Tanimoto first shared it with the teachers at Puohala Elementary.*

French Onion Dip

Yield: 2 cups

2 cups sour cream
½ cup mayonnaise
1 envelope Lipton® onion soup mix (2 oz.)

Combine all ingredients. Cover and chill. Serve with tortilla strips, crackers or vegetables.

☛ NOTE: *An old but ever popular dip at parties. So easy!*

Guacamole

Yield: about 1 cup

1 large ripe avocado, peeled and pitted
¼ small onion, finely chopped
½ tomato, seeded and diced
½ teaspoon lemon juice
1 tablespoon mayonnaise (optional)

Mash avocado to a coarse texture. Add rest of ingredients and mix thoroughly. Place plastic wrap directly on dip to keep color fresh; refrigerate 30 to 60 minutes before serving.

Kamaboko Dip

Yield: 1½ cups

1 kamaboko (6 oz.), grated or minced
¼ cup green onions, thinly sliced
4 tablespoons mayonnaise
4 water chestnuts, minced (optional)

Mix all ingredients together. Cover; refrigerate for 30 minutes. Serve with Ritz® crackers for a great tasting pupu.

Hot Crab Dip

Yield: 6 to 8 servings

1 package imitation crab, shredded (8 oz.)
1 cup mayonnaise
1 to 2 tablespoons onion, minced
¾ cup cheddar cheese, shredded

Mix together crab, mayonnaise and onion. Place in microwaveable dish (e.g., 9-inch glass pie pan). Top with cheese; microwave until cheese melts (about 2 minutes).

Serve hot with Ritz® crackers, warm French bread, etc.

☛ NOTE: *This is definitely the easiest hot crab dip! It's great just the way it is.*

Kamaboko and Crab Dip

Yield: 3½ cups

1 block kamaboko (6 oz.), minced
8 ounces imitation crab, shredded
¼ cup green onions, thinly sliced
1 cup sour cream
1 cup mayonnaise
Garlic salt and pepper, to taste

Mix all ingredients. Cover and refrigerate for 30 minutes. Serve with vegetables or crackers.

Kimchee Dip

Yield: 2 cups

½ cup kimchee, chopped
¼ cup onion, finely chopped
1 package cream cheese (8 oz.), softened
¼ cup mayonnaise

Mix ingredients together. Let sit for 20 minutes before serving.

☛ NOTE: *A great local favorite! The "Original High Max" brand for won-bok kimchee is highly recommended by my daughter, Jennifer.*

Macadamia Nut Cheese Ball

Yield: 12 servings

2 packages cream cheese (8 oz. each), softened
1½ cups cheddar cheese, finely shredded
½ cup sweet pickles, finely chopped
2 to 3 teaspoons onion, minced
1 teaspoon salt
½ cup macadamia nuts, finely chopped

Combine all ingredients (except macadamia nuts); mix well. Shape into a ball; roll in chopped nuts. Cover with plastic wrap and refrigerate several hours or until well-chilled. Serve with crackers.

☛ NOTE: *Very popular at gatherings. Tastes great and so easy to make!*

Spinach Dip

Yield: 2 cups

1 box frozen chopped spinach (9 oz.), thawed and squeezed dry
8 oz. sour cream, softened
1 package vegetable soup mix
(e.g., Lipton® Vegetable Soup and Dip Mix)
¾ cup mayonnaise
1 can water chestnuts (8 oz.), chopped
2 tablespoons green onions, chopped

Combine all ingredients. Refrigerate. Great with Ritz® crackers.

Finger Foods

Banana Lumpia

Yield: 30 pieces

15 short bananas (or 8 larger type bananas), firm and ripe
Brown sugar for sprinkling
1 package lumpia wrappers (16 oz.),
(e.g., Menlo® pastry wrapper)
Oil for frying

Defrost lumpia wrappers in refrigerator a day before using.

Peel bananas; cut in half lengthwise. (For longer bananas, first cut in half, then slice lengthwise.) Carefully separate lumpia wrappers; place a piece of banana on wrapper. Sprinkle about ½ teaspoon sugar on each banana. Wrap bananas in lumpia wrappers envelope style. Seal ends with dab of water. Heat about ½-inch oil in pan; fry both sides until golden brown. Drain on paper towels.

- NOTE: *A real local favorite! Watch it disappear quickly at any potluck.*

- VARIATION: *Lilian and Jerry McCellen suggests adding a pinch of cinnamon with brown sugar for added flavor. Also, for another great pupu, Jerry substitutes the bananas with cheese logs. Fantastic, he says.*

Aku or ʻAhi Poke

Yield: 4 to 6 appetizer servings

1 pound aku or ʻahi, cut in ¾-inch squares
1 teaspoon Hawaiian salt
1 teaspoon soy sauce
1 tablespoon water
1 teaspoon sesame oil (begin with less, adjust to taste)
¼ cup raw limu, chopped

Combine all ingredients; toss lightly. Refrigerate for at least 1 hour before serving.

Deviled Eggs

Yield: 24 pieces

12 large hard-boiled eggs, cooled
Mayonnaise to moisten
Curry powder to taste
Salt and white pepper to taste

Peel eggs and slice lengthwise. Pop the yolks out into food processor or bowl. (Keep the whites in a separate dish.) Add a dash of curry powder, salt and pepper to taste. Begin with less seasoning. Mash yolks or process until powdery. Mix in mayonnaise to make it like frosting consistency. Add more curry, salt or pepper as needed.

Fill a pastry bag fitted with a "star" tip and squeeze filling into egg whites. Or, if no pastry bag is available, just fill egg whites with spoonfuls of the yolk mixture.

☛ NOTE: *To get perfect boiled eggs: Place eggs in small saucepan; cover with water. Bring to boil, cover, and remove from heat. Let stand 10 minutes; drain and rinse with cold water.*

Boiled Peanuts, Chinese Style

Yield: 10 to 12 appetizer servings

1 pound raw peanuts
1 to 2 tablespoons salt
2 to 3 star anise

Rinse peanuts several times, or until water is clear. Cover peanuts with water. Add salt and star anise. Bring to boil. Lower heat and simmer, covered, for 1 to 2 hours, frequently stirring peanuts. Taste peanuts for doneness desired. Do not overcook.

☛ NOTE: *There are many varieties of peanuts. Some are better for roasting, others for boiling. Shop around for your favorite. I prefer the raw peanuts packaged by Exotic Food Distributors sold at Longs Store for this recipe.*

Cheese Quesadillas

Yield: 4 to 5 servings

5 flour tortillas, burrito size (10-inches round)
2½ cups shredded Monterey Jack or cheddar cheese, or combination

In large skillet, warm a tortilla for a few seconds over medium heat (Use no oil). Sprinkle about ½ cup cheese over half of the tortilla. Fold tortilla in half, pressing gently. Cook for 1 to 2 minutes on each side or until lightly brown and crisp to your taste. Remove and place on cutting board. Cut quesadillas into triangles.

☛ SUGGESTION: *Serve with guacamole or salsa.*

☛ NOTE: *So simple and easy to make. Children love it.*

Buffalo Wings

Yield: 8 to 10 pupu servings

½ cup butter (1 stick), melted
½ cup Tabasco® sauce
4 to 5 pounds chicken wings
1 teaspoon salt
4 to 5 cups vegetable oil, enough to cover chicken (about 1½ inches deep)
1 cup blue cheese dressing
2 celery stalks, cut in 2-inch lengths

Combine melted butter and Tabasco® sauce; set aside.

Rinse and pat dry chicken wings; sprinkle with salt. Heat oil on medium heat to 375° in deep pot. Deep fry chicken wings. Gently shake off excess oil and place about 4 to 5 pieces in Tabasco® sauce mixture. Coat all over and drain on paper towels. Serve with blue cheese dressing and celery sticks.

☛ NOTE: *Great taste! This is the best easy recipe yet. Recommended by Evelyn Shiraki whose son Mark loves it. My daughter Jennifer says "Yummy!"*

☛ HINT: *Use smaller-sized wings for best results. For another great recipe for buffalo wings, check out the recipe in my* Pupu and Potluck *cookbook.*

Namako (Konnyaku) Pūpū

Yield: 2 to 4 appetizer servings

1 cup namako, sliced or 2 pieces konnyaku, sliced
4 tablespoons sugar
4 tablespoons fresh lemon juice
1 teaspoon salt
1½ cup daikon, grated

Combine all ingredients. Refrigerate.

Cocktail Shrimp

Yield: 50 to 60 pieces

2 quarts water
1 bay leaf
Juice of one lemon
Rind of one lemon
1 can beer
2 pounds shrimp (31-40 size), peeled and deveined

Combine all ingredients (except shrimp), and bring water to aggressive boil. Add shrimp and stir, whirling through the boiling water. Cover tightly and remove from heat. Allow to stand for 5 minutes exactly. Then drain through colander. Run shrimp under cold water to cool. Chill and arrange on platter with dipping sauce.

Dipping Sauce:
1 cup ketchup
2 teaspoons wasabi paste
Juice of one lemon

☛ NOTE: *1 to 5 pounds of shrimp may be used with this recipe.*

Tako Poke

Yield: 4 to 6 appetizer servings

1 to 2 pounds cooked tako, thinly sliced diagonally
½ to 1 cup limu, chopped
2 pinches Hawaiian salt
2 pinches ʻinamona (optional)
Dash chili pepper water
¼ cup green onion, chopped
½ teaspoon sesame oil

Mix ingredients and adjust seasoning to your taste.

Kathy Morita's Korean Garlic Chicken Wings

Yield: 10 to 12 pupu servings

1 bag frozen chicken wing pieces (4 to 5 pounds),
(No need to defrost)
2 to 3 cups flour, for dredging chicken wings
Oil for deep-frying

Sauce:
1 cup low-sodium soy sauce
¾ cup sugar
2 tablespoons green onions, thinly sliced
1-inch piece fresh ginger root, grated
8 to 10 cloves garlic, minced (more or less to taste)
¼ teaspoon chili pepper flakes

Combine sauce ingredients in bowl; mix together to dissolve sugar. Set aside.

In large frying pan or pot, heat enough oil on medium heat to cover chicken. While oil is heating, place about 2 to 3 cups flour in large brown paper bag to dredge chicken. Rinse frozen chicken wings and drain. Place about 6 to 8 wings in bag to coat. When oil is hot enough, fry chicken wings until golden and crispy. Gently shake off excess oil and immediately place wings in sauce a few pieces at a time. Coat with sauce and place in serving dish.

☛ NOTE: *Great flavor! Thanks to Kathy Morita who shared her very popular pupu with us. Chicken may be eaten hot or cold. May be made day in advance and refrigerated after cooling.*

Furikake Seared 'Ahi

Yield: 4 to 6 appetizer servings

1 pound 'ahi fillet, sliced into ¾-inch thick pieces
3 to 4 tablespoons furikake, for coating
2 to 3 teaspoons oil

Dipping Sauce:
2 tablespoons soy sauce
Wasabi to taste

Coat entire 'ahi pieces with furikake. Sear 'ahi in hot oil in non-stick skillet on medium high heat, keeping the middle raw. Slice 'ahi in slices, sashimi style. Mix soy sauce and wasabi to desired taste and use as dipping sauce.

Spicy Edamame (Soybeans)

Yield: about 4 appetizer servings

1 pound frozen edamame
8 cups water
1 tablespoon salt
1 to 2 cloves garlic, minced
1 Hawaiian chili pepper, seeded and minced
1 to 2 tablespoons salt, to taste

Boil water and add salt. Place frozen edamame into salted boiling water. Bring to boil again and cook for a few minutes. Drain well and return to pot. While edamame is still hot, add rest of ingredients and toss until well-coated. Refrigerate overnight. Serve cold, or warm in microwave just before serving.

Easy Shrimp Skewers

Yield: about 30 skewers

3 pounds shrimp, 31-40 size
1 bottle Kraft® Zesty Italian dressing (16 oz.)
1 package barbecue skewers (8-inch skewers)

Shell and devein shrimp. Soak shrimp in Italian dressing 5 hours or longer in refrigerator. Skewer three shrimp in "C" shape with tail-side down on each stick. Cook on hibachi over coals.

Stuffed Celery

Yield: 15 to 18 pieces

3 stalks celery, cut into 1½-inch lengths
½ kamaboko, grated (half of 6.5 oz. package)
2 tablespoons mayonnaise
⅛ teaspoon sugar
Dash Worcestershire® sauce
1 teaspoon onion, finely chopped

Mix kamaboko with mayonnaise, sugar, Worcestershire® sauce and onion. Stuff celery and serve chilled.

Shoyu Poke

Yield: 4 to 6 appetizer servings

1 pound aku, cut in bite-size pieces
¼ cup green onion, chopped
½ teaspoon toasted sesame seeds
¼ cup soy sauce
1 teaspoon fresh ginger, grated
½ teaspoon inamona (optional)
1 Hawaiian chili pepper, seeded and minced

Combine all ingredients and mix well. Chill before serving.

Shrimp and Kamaboko Tempura

Yield: about 50 pieces

6 to 8 medium shrimp, cleaned and chopped
1 block kamaboko (6 oz.), chopped
1 cup water chestnuts, minced
1 stalk green onion, finely sliced
Oil for deep frying

Batter:

¾ cup flour
½ teaspoon salt
1 teaspoon sugar
1 egg, slightly beaten
¼ cup ice water

Combine flour, salt and sugar; set aside. In small bowl, combine egg and water; beat together. Add egg mixture into dry ingredients; stir only to moisten the dry ingredients. Add shrimp, kamaboko, water chestnut and green onion; mix well together. Drop by teaspoonfuls into heated oil. Fry until light brown. Serve hot.

- NOTE: *This is a great-tasting pupu dish that is fast and simple! May be served with hot mustard and soy sauce on the side.*

- SUGGESTION: *For safety, use 2 teaspoons: one to scoop the mixture and the other to scrape it off into the hot oil.*

Soups

uick & Easy

Alex's Quick Clam Chowder

Yield: 4 to 6 servings

1 can Progresso® Traditional New England Clam Chowder (18.5 oz.)
1 can Snow's® New England Clam Chowder, condensed (15 oz.)
1 can milk (Use Snow's® Clam Chowder can.)
1 can Snow's® Minced Clams (6.5 oz.), clam juice included

Combine all ingredients and cook on medium-low heat slowly, stirring occasionally.

☛ NOTE: *Very easy and very tasty! Thanks to Ruby Saito who got it from her friend, Alex, and shared it with me.*

☛ NOTE: *Do not use Snow's® Ready to Serve Clam Chowders.*

Black Bean Soup

Yield: 12 to 15 servings

2 cans whole-kernel corn (15 oz. each), drained
2 cans black beans (15 oz. each), drain only one can
2 cans diced tomatoes with green chilies (14.5 oz. each)
2 cans chicken broth (14.5 oz. each)
2 cans chunk chicken in water (10 oz. each), or meat from 1 roast chicken, chopped (about 3 cups)
Black pepper, to season

Combine all ingredients and bring to boil; simmer 5 minutes.

☛ NOTE: *This soup, a little on the spicy side, is quite popular with young adults. It is very tasty and so quick and easy to prepare. My young neighbor, Coreen Mijo, got this recipe from her friend Debbie Murata and shared it with me.*

Carrot Soup

Yield: 6 servings

1 pound carrots, sliced
1 large onion, diced
1 teaspoon oil
1 tablespoon curry powder
4 cups soup stock or vegetable broth

Sauté carrots, onion and curry powder in oil. Add soup broth. Cook 20 minutes. Place in blender and puree.

☛ SUGGESTION: *Serve with a dollop of sour cream or yogurt.*

Chinese Chicken Soup

Yield: 10 servings

1 skinless and boneless chicken breast (or 2 thighs), sliced
2 teaspoons cornstarch
1 teaspoon sesame oil
4 cans chicken broth (14.5 oz. each)
½ cup bamboo shoots, sliced
2 cups green vegetables, such as mustard cabbage, watercress, spinach, etc., cut into 2-inch lengths
Salt, to taste

Marinate chicken with cornstarch and sesame oil; set aside for 15 minutes. Heat broth until boiling; add chicken and cook for 3 minutes. Skim off froth. Add bamboo shoots and vegetables. Cook until vegetables are done. Taste and add salt, if necessary.

Chicken-Tomato Soup

Yield: 12 to 14 servings

2 cans chicken broth (15 oz. each)
2 cans stewed tomatoes (14.5 oz. each), chopped
1 can pinto beans (15 oz.)
1 cup salsa, any brand (adjust to taste)
1 can whole kernel corn (7 oz.)
1 can sliced black olives (2.25 oz.), drained
2 tablespoons basil
1 teaspoon cumin

Combine ingredients in pot. Bring to boil and simmer for approximately 1 hour.

Pork and Mustard Cabbage Soup

Yield: 4 servings

½ cup lean pork, thinly sliced
2 teaspoons oil
Hawaiian salt and pepper to taste
2 cans chicken broth (14.5 oz. each)
½ cup water
½ pound mustard cabbage, chopped in 1-inch pieces

Season pork slices with a light sprinkle of Hawaiian salt and pepper. Heat oil and pork; fry until lightly browned. Add chicken broth and water. Bring to boil, lower heat and simmer about 15 minutes. Add mustard cabbage and simmer, uncovered, until tender (about 7 minutes).

☛ NOTE: *Here is a soup suggested by Glennis Ooka that will have your keiki enjoy mustard cabbage! My granddaughter, Kristen, who resists eating anything green, will eat the mustard cabbage if it is cooked in this way.*

Clam Soup

Yield: 4 servings

1 can boiled baby clams (10 oz.), (e.g., Shirakiku® brand)
1 can water (use clams can)
1 can chicken broth (14.5 oz.)
Mustard cabbage or won bok, cut into bite-size pieces

Pour can of boiled clams, with liquid, into saucepan. Add water and chicken broth; heat. When soup begins to boil, add desired amount of mustard cabbage leaves. Cook until softened.

Egg Flower Pea Soup

Yield: 6 servings

½ pound ground pork
2 slices fresh ginger, crushed
5 cups water
1 can peas (17 oz.), DO NOT DRAIN
1 teaspoon salt
1 to 2 eggs, beaten

Brown pork. Add ginger and water. Bring to boil; skim off froth and oil. Lower heat and simmer 20 minutes. Remove ginger slices and add can of peas with liquid and salt. Bring to boil again. Stir in egg. Serve immediately.

☛ NOTE: *This is a variation of an old favorite pea soup that my husband, Don, enjoyed. It had to be canned peas for this soup.*

Fresh Mushroom Soup

Yield: 6 to 8 servings

1 medium onion, chopped
1 container fresh button mushrooms (8 oz.), sliced
2 tablespoons margarine or butter
3 tablespoons flour
2 cans chicken broth (14½ oz. each)
Pepper to taste
1 can evaporated milk (12 oz.)

Sauté onion and mushrooms in margarine until softened. Add flour and stir to coat. Add broth and pepper; stir and simmer, covered, for 10 minutes. Add milk; blend well. Heat and serve.

Imitation Bird Nest Soup

Yield: 5 to 6 servings

1 bundle long rice (2 oz.), soaked in hot water for 30 minutes
4 shiitake mushrooms, soaked in water to soften
1 cup bamboo shoots, thinly sliced
3 cans chicken broth (14.5 oz. each)
½ cup pork, thinly sliced
½ cup ham, thinly sliced
2 eggs, beaten
½ cup green onions, thinly sliced
Salt, to taste

Drain long rice and cut into approximately ½-inch pieces. Drain mushrooms, discard stems and slice mushrooms into thin strips. Combine long rice, mushrooms, bamboo shoots and broth; bring to boil. Add pork and ham; simmer for 15 to 20 minutes. Just before serving, stir in beaten eggs and green onions.

☛ VARIATION: *Substitute green onions with Chinese parsley. Substitute bamboo shoots with ½ cup chopped water chestnuts.*

Garden Vegetable Soup

Yield: 6 to 8 servings

1 small onion, diced
4 cloves garlic, minced
1 large carrot, sliced diagonally (about 1½ cups)
3 cans chicken broth (14 oz. each)
3 cups cabbage, diced
1 package green beans (8 oz.), cut into 1 to 1½-inch pieces
2 tablespoons tomato paste (more or less to taste)
1 teaspoon dried basil
½ teaspoon dried oregano
½ teaspoon salt
1 small zucchini, diced

In large pot, heat 1 to 2 teaspoons oil (or use nonstick cooking spray). Sauté onion and garlic over medium-low heat; add carrot, cover and continue cooking until softened, about 5 minutes. Add rest of ingredients, except zucchini, and bring to boil. Lower heat and simmer, covered, until beans are tender, about 15 minutes. Stir in zucchini and cook 3 to 4 minutes longer.

☛ NOTE: *This is a great soup for anyone wanting to cut down on the amount of calories eaten at a meal. Begin with this tasty soup as a first course. My neighbor, Evelyn Shiraki, shared this recipe and we all love it.*

Easy Egg Flower Drop Soup

Yield: 6 servings

2 cans chicken broth (14.5 oz. each)
1 can cream-style corn (14.75 oz.)
1 egg, beaten

Heat chicken broth; stir in corn. Bring to boil; stir in beaten egg.

☛ NOTE: *Glenn Oura, who lives in Maui, shared this easy recipe with me.*

Jiffy Clam Chowder

Yield: 4 servings

1 can chopped or minced clams (6.5 oz.), DO NOT DRAIN
1 cup skim milk
½ teaspoon minced onion flakes
Salt and pepper, to taste
1 crown cauliflower, chopped (about 3 cups)

Combine all ingredients (except cauliflower). Cover and simmer for 5 minutes. Add chopped cauliflower. Cook for 25 minutes more or until cauliflower is softened.

Kimchee Soup

Yield: 4 servings

8 to 10 ounces ground pork or thinly sliced lean pork
3 slices fresh ginger
3 cans chicken broth (14.5 oz. each)
1 bottle kimchee (12 oz.), (e.g., Kohala® Wòn-Bok Kimchee), include liquid
1½ pounds winter melon (togan), cut into 1½" x 2½" (about 15 pieces)
1 block firm tofu (20 oz.), cut into 1-inch cubes

Brown ground pork with ginger; drain oil. Add chicken broth. Chop kimchee into smaller pieces and, together with kimchee liquid, add to soup. Add wintermelon and simmer for 15 to 20 minutes or until wintermelon becomes soft. Add tofu and cook about 1 to 2 minutes more.

☛ NOTE: *Lessen amount of kimchee if it is too hot for your taste.*

Miso Soup

Yield: 6 to 8 servings

6 cups water
½ cup dried shrimp
½ cup miso, blended with ¼ cup water
1 block tofu (14 oz.), cut into cubes
¼ cup green onions, thinly sliced (for garnish)

Boil shrimp in water for 20 minutes. Strain and discard shrimp. Bring shrimp-flavored water to boil again. Add blended miso and simmer 10 to 15 minutes. Add tofu; cook until tofu is heated through. Serve in soup bowls and garnish with green onions.

☛ NOTE: *This is a favorite soup of my grandchildren. Whenever their mother serves salmon for dinner, she also prepares this simple soup to go with the meal. Feeling under the weather? Miso soup is great!*

Jiffy Corn Chowder

Quick & Easy

Yield: 5 to 6 servings

1 can chicken broth (14.5 oz.)
1 can cream of potato soup (10¾ oz.)
1 can cream of celery soup (10¾ oz.)
1 can cream-style corn, no salt (14¾ oz.)

Combine soups; blend together. Add corn and stir well. Heat over medium heat for 15 minutes.

Oxtail Soup with Red Beans

Yield: 5 to 6 servings

1 tray oxtail (about 2 pounds)
¾ cup dried small red beans, soaked overnight in 2½ cups water
1 onion, chopped
2 tomatoes, chopped
2 cloves, crushed
Salt and pepper, to taste
1 bay leaf (optional)

Parboil oxtail (about 20 minutes); drain and rinse. Trim off fat, if necessary. Lightly scrub pot to remove. Place oxtail back in pot, cover with water and bring to boil. Drain red beans which have been soaked overnight, and add to soup. Add rest of ingredients. Simmer, occasionally skimming off fat, until oxtail is soft (about 3 hours or more).

- NOTE: *Merv Chun, who is a great cook, shared this recipe as an easy soup to prepare. It just takes time to simmer oxtail until it is so tender that the meat falls off the bone. Tastes even better the next day.*

- VARIATION: *Merv suggests using more red beans, if desired. He says that after the oxtail is eaten, he enjoys the broth with beans over rice.*

Tofu Zucchini Soup

Yield: 4 to 5 servings

2 cans chicken broth (14.5 oz. each)
1 to 2 medium zucchini, cut ½-inch rounds or half circles
½ block firm tofu (half of 20 oz.), cut into 1-inch cubes
Salt and pepper, to taste

Bring broth to boil. Add zucchini and cook 5 minutes. Add tofu and simmer, covered, for 5 minutes. Garnish with green onions.

Egg Flower Soup

Yield: 4 servings

3 to 4 tablespoons instant chicken bouillon, dissolved in 1 quart hot water
½ cup water chestnuts, finely chopped
2 eggs beaten
¼ teaspoon pepper (or less, to taste)

Heat chicken broth, covered, until boiling. Add water chestnuts; simmer, covered, for 5 minutes. Add beaten eggs slowly, continually stirring. Add pepper.

☛ VARIATION: *Add ½ cup mushrooms, diced, with water chestnuts.*

Vegetarian Corn Chowder

Yield: 6 to 8 servings

1 large potato, peeled and cubed (about 2 cups)
2 cups water
1 teaspoon salt
½ teaspoon celery salt
½ teaspoon parsley flakes
1½ stalks celery, diced (about 1 cup)
½ cup onion, chopped
1 bay leaf
1 can cream-style corn (14.75 oz.)
1 can corn niblets (11 oz.)
2 cups soy milk (more or less)

Place all ingredients (except last three) in large pot; simmer over low heat until potatoes are almost done (about 5 to 10 minutes). Stir in niblets and cream-style corn and simmer 10 minutes, stirring frequently. Add soy milk to desired consistency. Turn heat off and let stand 15 to 20 minutes. Remove bay leaf before serving.

NOTE: *I had never used soy milk until Nancy Ishikawa gave me this recipe. Not only is this soup very delicious but I also learned to use and enjoy soy milk in place of my lactaid milk.*

Watercress Egg-Drop Soup

Yield: 4 servings

2 cans chicken broth (14.5 oz. each)
1 clove garlic, lightly crushed
2 thin slices fresh ginger
1 bunch watercress, coarsely chopped about 1½-inch in length
1 egg, lightly beaten

Combine first three ingredients in medium saucepan; bring to boil Add watercress and simmer until softened. Add egg, stirring, until egg is lightly cooked. Remove garlic and ginger slices. Serve immediately.

Salads

Bean Salad

Yield: 8 to 10 servings

3 or more kinds of canned beans (e.g., green, yellow wax, kidney, soy, garbanzo), drained well
1 medium Maui onion, thinly sliced
1 can whole mushrooms (6.5 oz.), drained
1 green pepper, sliced (optional)
1 can young corn, whole spears (15 oz.), (optional)

Marinade:
¼ cup sugar
⅔ cup vinegar
⅓ cup Wesson® oil
1 teaspoon salt

Marinate ingredients in marinade. Best if prepared a day or more before serving.

☛ NOTE: *Here is another "oldie but goodie" recipe from my Puohala Elementary School days in the 1970s. Thanks to Ethel Nishida who shared this recipe with us.*

Spinach and Feta Pasta Salad

Yield: 6 servings

1 box penne pasta, (8 oz.), cooked according to box directions (Drain and set aside for 15 minutes)
1 bunch fresh spinach (about 4 to 5 cups), discard stems
1 cup quartered cherry tomatoes (or raisin tomatoes)
½ cup green onions, chopped
1 container Athenos® Feta Cheese with Basil and Tomatoes (4 oz.), crumbled
2 tablespoons olive oil

Mix all ingredients. Cover and refrigerate until chilled.

☛ NOTE: *Delicious! This is a great-tasting salad.*

Bean Sprout Salad

Yield: 4 to 5 servings

1 bag bean sprouts (10 oz.)

Parboil briefly until just slightly soft. Drain and rinse in cold water. Drain and set aside.

Dressing:

1 tablespoon vinegar
2 tablespoons soy sauce
2 to 3 teaspoons sesame oil
1 clove garlic, crushed
¼ green onions, thinly sliced
Salt and pepper to taste

Mix together dressing ingredients. Place drained bean sprouts in bowl and pour dressing over. Toss gently; chill.

Carrot Raisin Salad

Yield: 4 servings

1 cup carrot, grated
1 cup cabbage, shredded
¼ cup raisins
½ teaspoon salt
1 tablespoon sugar
2 tablespoons lemon juice (about 1 lemon)
¼ cup mayonnaise

Toss together carrot, cabbage, raisins, salt, sugar and lemon juice. Refrigerate until ready to serve. Just before serving, add mayonnaise and toss together.

☛ NOTE: *Very good! Don't let the title stop you from trying this tasty salad.*

Broccoli with Sunflower Seeds

Yield: 4 to 6 servings

2 stalks broccoli, cut into small bite-sized pieces
1 cup dry roasted sunflower seeds, or less
½ cup raisins
1 stalk green onions, thinly sliced (about ¼ cup)

Dressing:
1 cup mayonnaise
½ cup sugar
2 tablespoon apple cider vinegar

Mix dressing ingredients together, blending well; set aside.

Combine broccoli, sunflower seeds, raisins and green onions. Pour dressing over and toss together. Refrigerate.

- NOTE: *Love this salad! I've had a similar broccoli salad at the Sky Garden Restaurant at Imiloa in Hilo and everyone liked it there.*

- HINT: *No need to parboil broccoli. I also peel the stalks and cut them into thin slices and add them into the salad. Thanks to Evelyn Shiraki for sharing her recipe with me so I can share it with you.*

Broccoli Salad

Yield: 3 to 4 servings

2 stalks broccoli, cut into bite-sized pieces and blanched
5 to 6 ounces imitation crab, coarsely shredded
Mayonnaise, to blend
Salt and pepper, to taste
1 tablespoon lemon juice (optional)

Mix all ingredients together. Refrigerate.

Cauliflower and Broccoli Salad

Yield: 8 servings

1 head cauliflower, cut into bite-sized pieces
1 stalk broccoli, cut into bite-sized pieces
6 to 8 imitation crabmeat sticks, sliced into thirds and shredded
⅔ cup mayonnaise
Salt and pepper to taste
3 tablespoons green onion, thinly sliced (optional)

Parboil cauliflower and broccoli separately; rinse in cold water. Drain well. In large bowl, combine vegetables and crab; toss. Add mayonnaise; mix together. Season with salt and pepper. Add green onion, if desired. Refrigerate.

☛ NOTE: *Begin with less than ⅔ cup mayonnaise and add more to taste. Tastes even better when refrigerated several hours.*

Tuna on a Shoestring

Yield: 5 servings

1 can tuna (6 oz.), drained
½ cup carrot, shredded
1 cup celery, diced
¼ cup onion, minced
¾ cup mayonnaise
2 cups shoestring potatoes
Manoa or iceberg lettuce, rinsed, dried, and chilled

Place tuna in bowl and shred with fork. Add carrot, celery, onion and mayonnaise. Toss until coated. Cover and chill at least 2 hours. Just before serving, fold in shoestring potatoes. Serve on lettuce leaves on individual plates.

☛ NOTE: *Shoestring Potato sticks are sold in 7 oz. cans. The shoestring potatoes give this salad a very crispy and crunchy texture.*

Chicken Cucumber Salad

Yield: 6 to 8 servings

3 to 4 boneless and skinless chicken, cooked and shredded
4 to 5 cucumbers, cut into 2-inch strips
2 stalks green onions, thinly sliced

Sauce:
½ cup sugar
½ cup Japanese vinegar
¼ cup sesame oil
2 teaspoons Hondashi
½ cup soy sauce
3 tablespoons sesame seeds
2 cloves garlic, minced

Combine sauce ingredients; refrigerate. Refrigerate chicken, cucumbers and green onions. When ready to serve, mix everything together.

Cole Slaw

Yield: 4 servings

3 cups cabbage, shredded

Dressing:
¼ cup mayonnaise
1 teaspoon onion, minced
1 tablespoon sugar
1½ teaspoons vinegar
1½ teaspoons prepared yellow mustard
¼ teaspoon salt
Celery seeds for sprinkling

Mix together dressing ingredients; pour over shredded cabbage and toss together. Refrigerate and serve chilled.

Easy Caesar Salad

Yield: Serves 6 as a side dish

1 head Romaine lettuce, torn into bite-sized pieces
1 cup croutons
½ cup Caesar salad dressing (use your favorite brand)
2 to 3 tablespoons Parmesan cheese, grated (adjust to taste)

Place lettuce in large salad bowl. Add croutons and dressing; toss lightly. Sprinkle with Parmesan cheese.

☛ NOTE: *This is a quick and tasty salad to prepare when you are busy. Just be sure that the Romaine lettuce is chilled and crisp.*

Tofu Salad

Yield: 10 servings

1 block tofu (20 oz.), cubed
½ Maui onion, thinly sliced
1 can salmon (7.5 oz.)
½ bag bean sprouts, (half of 10 oz. bag)
4 to 5 cups watercress, cut in ½-inch pieces
1 tomato, cut in bite-sized pieces
¼ cup green onions, thinly sliced

Dressing:
1 cup soy sauce
½ cup vegetable oil

Combine soy sauce and oil; heat. Set aside to cool.

Layer salad ingredients in bowl in order given; refrigerate. Just before serving, shake dressing well and drizzle desired amount over salad.

☛ NOTE: *Another version of the very popular tofu salad. This was shared by Terrie Osorno, who works at Borders in Maui. Her dressing uses less ingredients and the bean sprouts are not parboiled so that makes it easier to prepare.*

Tuna Macaroni Salad

Yield: 8 to 10 servings

2 cups uncooked macaroni
4 medium potatoes
1 package frozen peas (10 oz.)
5 to 6 hard-cooked eggs, cut into bite-sized pieces
¼ onion, finely diced
¼ cup celery, finely diced
2 tablespoons sweet pickle relish
1 can tuna (6 oz.), drained
1 cup mayonnaise, adjust to just moisten ingredients
Salt and pepper, to taste

Boil macaroni in salted water until tender; drain and cool. Peel potatoes; cut into bite-sized pieces and boil in salted water until tender. Drain and cool. Defrost peas in half-inch of salted hot water; drain. In small bowl, combine together diced onion, celery and sweet pickle relish; set aside. In large bowl, mix all ingredients to create desired consistency. Season with salt and pepper. Refrigerate, covered, until serving time.

Chicken or Turkey Salad

Yield: 4 to 6 servings

2 cups cooked cold chicken (thighs or breasts), or turkey, cut in cubes
2 stalks celery, chopped (about 1 cup)
2 hard-boiled eggs, chopped
1 tablespoon lemon juice
½ cup mayonnaise (Begin with less and adjust to taste)
Salt and pepper, to taste
Tomato wedges or slices for garnish (optional)

Mix all ingredients together; chill. Serve on lettuce; garnish with tomatoes, if desired.

Easy French Dressing

Yield: 2 cups

1 cup oil
¾ cup sugar
⅓ cup vinegar
¾ cup ketchup
Pepper, to taste (optional)
1 clove garlic, minced (optional)

Combine ingredients; blend well with whisk. Refrigerate.

Sesame-Hoi Sin Dressing

Yield: 1 cups

⅓ cup sesame oil
2 tablespoons hoi sin sauce
2 tablespoons vinegar
¼ cup sugar
¼ cup ketchup
1 teaspoon salt

Combine and mix well.

☛ NOTE: *This is my cousin, Judy Takabayashi's favorite dressing.*

Sides

Bell Pepper Sauté

Yield: 4 servings

2 bell peppers, red or yellow
1 tablespoon olive oil
½ small red onion, chopped
Hawaiian salt and ground pepper, to taste
Fresh herbs (e.g., basil, dill, Chinese parsley, etc.)

Cut peppers in half; remove seeds and ribs. Cut lengthwise into strips and halve crosswise. Heat oil in large non-stick skillet over medium heat. Add bell peppers and onion. Season with salt and ground pepper. Cook until bell peppers are just tender. Stir occasionally. Just before serving, toss in chopped fresh herbs.

Broccoli Casserole

Yield: 8 servings

1 box frozen chopped broccoli (16 oz.), thawed
½ onion, chopped
¾ cup mayonnaise
1 can cream of mushroom soup (10¾ oz.)
1 egg, beaten
¾ cup sharp cheddar cheese, grated
12 to 14 Ritz® crackers, crumbled (optional)
2 tablespoons butter, melted

Place broccoli in greased (butter or non-stick spray) 2-quart casserole dish. Mix remaining ingredients; pour over broccoli. Sprinkle crumbled Ritz® crackers over, then glaze with melted butter. (If crackers are not used, butter.) Cover and bake at 350° for 30 minutes.

NOTE: *May be prepared ahead and refrigerated; bake for 45 minutes.*

Choi Sum

Yield: 3 to 4 servings

1 bunch choi sum (about ¾ pound)
1 tablespoon oil
2 cloves garlic, crushed
Hawaiian salt, to taste
½ cup water
1 tablespoon oyster sauce (optional)

Wash choi sum and cut into 3-inch lengths. Heat skillet on medium high, add oil and stir-fry garlic until lightly browned. Add choi sum; stir-fry until wilted and bright green in color. Sprinkle salt and add ½ cup water. Cover, lower heat, and cook about 2 to 3 minutes or until choi sum is tender. Stir occasionally. Mix in oyster sauce, if desired.

☛ VARIATION: *Substitute choi sum with other vegetables such as mustard cabbage, asparagus, broccoli, etc.*

Eggplant Parmigiana

Yield: 5 to 6 servings

1 round eggplant
1 can tomato sauce (8 oz.)
Mozzarella cheese, shredded, for topping
Oregano for sprinkling

Slice eggplant in round slices ½-inch thick and place in foil-lined flat pan. Pour tomato sauce over, top with Mozzarella and sprinkle oregano over. Bake at 350° for 30 minutes, or until cheese is slightly brown and eggplant is soft.

Green Beans and Pork

Yield: 6 to 8 servings

1 pound green beans, julienned
½ to 1 pound pork, thinly sliced

Sauce:

¼ cup low-salt soy sauce
2 tablespoons brown sugar
1 clove garlic, diced
1 teaspoon roasted sesame seeds
1 tablespoon green onion, chopped
Pepper, to season

Combine sauce ingredients and marinate pork for 15 to 20 minutes. In frying pan, fry pork together with sauce ingredients and simmer until pork is cooked. Add green beans and continue cooking, uncovered, until beans are tender. Stir occasionally.

Green Bean Casserole

Yield: 8 servings

2 cans cut green beans (14.5 oz each), drained
1 can Durkee's® French Fried Onions (2.8 oz.), reserve ¼ cup
1 can cream of mushroom soup (10¾ oz.)
Dash pepper
1 can mushrooms, pieces and stems (6.5 oz.), with liquid
½ cup toasted slivered almonds (or less)
⅔ cup cheddar cheese, grated

Mix first 6 ingredients (minus the reserved ¼ cup French-fried onions) together in bowl. Place in 2-quart casserole dish. Sprinkle the reserved ¼ cup French-fried onions over. Then sprinkle the cheddar cheese over all. Bake at 375° for 30 minutes.

☛ NOTE: *This is my daughter's favorite side dish for Thanksgiving!*

Green Beans with Miso Sauce

Yield: 6 servings

1 pound green beans, cut into 1½-inch pieces.

Sauce:
⅓ cup mayonnaise
2½ tablespoons miso
½ tablespoon sugar, adjust to taste
1½ tablespoons toasted sesame seeds

Parboil green beans until tender (about 5 to 10 minutes). Drain and cool. Combine sauce ingredients. Mix beans into sauce. Chill for 1 hour.

Grilled Asparagus

Yield: 4 to 5 servings

1 pound asparagus, tough bottom ends snapped off
1 to 2 tablespoons olive oil
Hawaiian salt, to taste
Pepper, to taste
Lemon juice, to taste (optional)

Marinate asparagus in olive oil; set aside. Heat large skillet until very hot. (Cast iron or grill pan is best.) Add marinated asparagus; cook, turning over with tongs until just tender (about 4 minutes). Lower heat, sprinkle with salt and pepper. Transfer to platter. Squeeze lemon juice over, if desired. Serve hot.

☛ NOTE: *Very healthy and tasty! A great side dish to many entrees.*

Kimpira Gobo

Yield: 3 to 4 servings

½ pound gobo, scraped clean,
slivered and soaked in water 20 minutes
1 tablespoon oil
1 tablespoon dried shrimp, minced
1 tablespoon sugar
3 tablespoons soy sauce
½ Hawaiian chili pepper (optional)

Drain gobo. Heat oil and sauté shrimp. Add gobo; cook for a few minutes, stirring occasionally. Add remaining ingredients and cook until sauce is absorbed. Add chili pepper, if desired. Do not overcook.

Korean Potatoes

Yield: 6 servings

3 medium potatoes (about 2 pounds)
2 cups water
1 tablespoon Hawaiian salt

Soy sauce Mixture:
1 cup water
¼ cup sugar
¼ cup low sodium soy sauce
1 tablespoon garlic, minced
½ teaspoon pepper
1 tablespoon oil

Peel and cut potatoes into bite-sized pieces. Immerse in brine of water and salt for 10 minutes; drain. Place potatoes in skillet and pour soy sauce mixture over. Cook, uncovered, on medium high for 10 to 20 minutes or until tender, stirring occasionally.

Maui Onion

Yield: 2 quarts

2½ pounds onions (about 6 onions), cut into quarters
2 to 4 Hawaiian chili peppers, crushed

Sauce:

½ cup sugar
1 handful Hawaiian salt
1¼ cups cider vinegar

Place onions and 1 to 2 chili peppers in each quart jar. Mix sauce ingredients and pour over onions. Let stand overnight, then refrigerate.

Ong Choy and Harm Ha

Yield: 4 servings

1 bunch ong choy (about 1 pound), rinsed and cut into 2-inch lengths
1 tablespoon oil
1 clove garlic, crushed
Hawaiian salt, to taste
½ cup water
1½ teaspoons harm ha (adjust to taste)

Heat oil and sauté garlic. Add ong choy and cook about 3 minutes, stirring occasionally. Add Hawaiian salt and water. Cover and simmer about 2 minutes. Add harm ha and continue cooking, uncovered, until ong choy is tender. Stir occasionally.

Special Spinach

Yield: 6 to 8 servings

2 packages frozen chopped spinach (8 oz. each)
¼ cup water
1 cup small curd cottage cheese
1½ tablespoons dry onion soup mix (adjust to taste)

Cook spinach in water just until tender. (Do not salt water.) Drain thoroughly, pressing out liquid. Put spinach in saucepan and stir in cottage cheese and onion soup mix. Cook over low heat, stirring occasionally, until mixture is hot.

Sesame Asparagus

Yield: 4 to 5 servings

1 pound asparagus
1 tablespoon oil
1 tablespoon vinegar
1 tablespoon soy sauce
4 teaspoons sugar
1 tablespoon roasted sesame seeds

Parboil or steam asparagus. Drain and place on platter. Heat remaining ingredients. Bring to boil and pour over asparagus.

☛ VARIATION: *Broccoli may be substituted for asparagus.*

Vietnamese Pickled Turnip and Carrot Strips

Yield: 2 cups

1 small carrot, peeled and julienned (about 1 cup)
1 small long turnip (daikon), peeled and julienned (about 1 cup)
¼ cup vinegar
¼ cup sugar
½ teaspoon salt

Place carrot and daikon strips into bowl. Add rest of ingredients and mix well. Let sit 30 minutes. Store in refrigerator. Squeeze liquid out before using in sandwiches.

☛ NOTE: *For easier shredding, check any Asian store and look for a hand grater that looks like a wide vegetable peeler with a waffle blade. Use it also to make green papaya salad.*

Roasted Vegetables

Yield: 4 to 5 servings

1 pound green beans (or asparagus, broccoli, squash, pumpkin slices, etc.)
1 to 2 tablespoons olive oil
Salt and pepper, to taste

Toss vegetables with olive oil. Season with salt and pepper. Place on cookie sheet. Bake at 400° on top third shelf of oven until lightly browned (about 15 minutes). Check after 10 minutes for doneness.

☛ SUGGESTION: *Serve with Miso Dip Dressing*

½ cup mayonnaise
½ teaspoon sugar
4 teaspoons Japanese rice vinegar
1 tablespoon white miso
1½ tablespoons peanut butter
½ teaspoon fresh ginger, grated
½ teaspoon garlic, grated or pressed
2 teaspoons sesame oil
1 teaspoon roasted sesame seeds

Mix dressing ingredients in the order listed. Refrigerate.

☛ NOTE: *Thanks to Ardis Ono in Hilo who shared this recipe with me and many others. The Miso Dip Dressing also tastes great with fresh raw vegetables.*

Spinach Casserole

Yield: 8 servings

2 boxes frozen spinach, thawed and drained (9 oz. each)
1 can cream of mushroom soup (10¾ oz.)
¾ cup mayonnaise
2 teaspoons onion soup mix
2 eggs, slightly beaten
Grated cheddar cheese for sprinkling

Squeeze excess water from drained spinach. Mix together with remaining ingredients (except cheddar cheese). Place in greased 1-quart casserole dish. Sprinkle desired amount of cheddar cheese over. Bake, covered, at 350° for 45 minutes.

Potato Pancakes

Yield: 8 patties

2 pounds potatoes (about 2 large potatoes)
1 egg
⅓ cup onion, finely chopped
3 tablespoons flour
1 teaspoon salt
¼ cup butter (½ stick)

Shred potatoes to 4 cups shredded potatoes (Place in container of water as you are shredding); drain. Beat egg in bowl. Squeeze out excess water from shredded potatoes and place in bowl. Mix in onion, flour and salt. Melt butter in skillet. Form potato mixture into patties, squeezing out excess water again and fry until browned on both sides. Add more butter, if needed.

☛ NOTE: *Another great tasting recipe from Merv Chun!*

Yatsumi Zuke

Yield: 2½ quarts

1 medium-sized head cabbage (about 2 pounds), chopped into ½-inch size
3 medium-sized mustard cabbage (about 2 pounds), chopped into ½-inch size
¼ cup Hawaiian salt
2 tablespoons roasted white sesame seeds

Sauce:
⅓ cup soy sauce
¼ cup Japanese vinegar
¼ cup brown sugar (firmly packed)
Hawaiian chili pepper, with or without seeds (optional)

Place both chopped cabbages in large container; add Hawaiian salt and mix well. Let set for 30 minutes. Drain and squeeze excess water and place back in container. Add sesame seeds.

Combine sauce ingredients and bring to boil. Pour the hot sauce over cabbage; mix well. Leave at room temperature for 3 to 4 hours, occasionally mixing. Place in jars and refrigerate.

☛ NOTE: *This recipe is for Judy Kodani Takabayashi's family. They loved her "yatsumi zuke"! Now they can make it themselves and remember Judy.*

Main Dishes

Asparagus with Beef

Yield: 8 servings

1 pound top round boneless (or sirloin or flank steak), thinly sliced
2 pounds asparagus, cut into 1½-inch diagonal slices
2 tablespoons oil
1 clove garlic, crushed
½ teaspoon salt
1 cup chicken broth
1 tablespoon cornstarch blended with 1 tablespoon water

Marinade:
1 tablespoon cornstarch
1 tablespoon soy sauce
¾ teaspoon sugar

Mix together marinade ingredients; add meat and marinate for 15 minutes. Parboil asparagus for 2 minutes; drain.

Heat oil on medium high heat; brown garlic. Add marinated beef; stir-fry, sprinkling salt over. When beef looks half done, add asparagus; stir-fry another 2 minutes. Add chicken broth; bring to boil and add cornstarch blended with water, mixing well.

Ground Beef with Salsa

Yield: 2 to 3 servings

1 pound ground beef
1 cup salsa, any brand (more or less to your taste)

Brown ground beef. Add salsa; cook until heated through. Serve over hot rice.

NOTE: *After a wedding party, Eleanor Tokunaga was given a huge container of leftover salsa. She experimented with the above and to her surprise, found it to be very tasty! Try it. I think you'll like it, too.*

Easy Beef Stroganoff

Yield: 4 servings

1 package egg noodles (12 oz.)
1 pound flank or sirloin steak, thinly sliced
½ onion, chopped
1 clove garlic, minced
¼ cup butter
2 teaspoons flour
½ teaspoon salt
¼ teaspoon pepper
1 can mushrooms, pieces and stems (6 oz.) (Do not drain.)
1 can cream of mushroom soup (10¾ oz.)
½ cup sour cream (optional)

Cook egg noodles according to package directions.

Sauté onions and garlic with butter. Add meat and simmer until tender. Add rest of ingredients; simmer 10 minutes. Pour over cooked noodles.

☛ NOTE: *Highly recommended! So delicious and so easy to prepare.*

Sloppy Joe

Yield: 4 servings

1 pound ground beef
2 tablespoons onion, chopped
2 tablespoons green pepper, chopped
2 tablespoons celery, chopped
1 can tomato sauce (8 oz.)
½ cup barbecue sauce (any brand)
Salt and pepper, to taste (optional)

Brown ground beef (no oil necessary). Drain excess oil. Stir in onion, green pepper and celery. Cook 2 to 3 minutes. Stir in tomato sauce and barbecue sauce. Add salt and pepper if desired. Cover and simmer about 15 minutes, stirring occasionally. Serve over rice or hamburger buns.

Barbecued Meatballs

Yield: 4 servings

1 pound ground beef
¼ cup uncooked oatmeal
1 teaspoon salt
⅛ teaspoon pepper
⅓ cup milk (or less)
2 tablespoons oil

Mix all ingredients (except oil); form into balls. Heat oil and brown meatballs; place in saucepan. Set aside.

Sauce:

½ cup ketchup
2 tablespoons brown sugar
2 tablespoons vinegar
1 tablespoon soy sauce
1 tablespoon Worcestershire® Sauce
2 teaspoons yellow mustard

Combine sauce ingredients and pour over meatballs. Cover and simmer until meatballs are done (about 30 minutes).

☛ NOTE: *A favorite with children! When doubling the amount of meatballs, not necessary to double sauce.*

Beef and Snow Peas

Yield: 4 to 6 servings

1 pound sirloin steak, thinly sliced
2 tablespoons peanut oil
25 snow peas, ends and strings removed
12 water chestnuts, sliced (about ½ cup)

Marinade:
1 tablespoon cornstarch
1 tablespoon sherry
3 tablespoons soy sauce
1 teaspoon sugar

Mix together marinade ingredients; add meat and marinate 15 minutes. Heat oil on medium-high heat. Add marinated meat and stir-fry 2 minutes. Add rest of ingredients; stir-fry 1 minute.

Cream of Mushroom Meatballs

Yield: 5 to 6 servings

1 onion, diced
1 pound ground beef
2 to 4 slices bread, crumbled
2 eggs
2 cans cream of mushroom soup (10¾ oz. each)
Soy sauce, to taste
Salt and pepper, to taste
Oil

Heat oil and sauté onions; set aside to cool. In bowl, mix ground beef, bread and eggs. Add cooked onions, salt and pepper; mix thoroughly. Roll ground beef mixture into meatballs. Fry meatballs in oil and drain fat. Mix in cream of mushroom; add enough soy sauce to add color to gravy. Let simmer for 10 minutes. Serve over hot rice.

☛ NOTE: *Everyone loves this! Tastes even better the next day.*

Easy Tripe Stew

Yield: 4 servings

1 pound honeycormb tripe
1 to 2 tablespoons baking soda
1 small onion, cut in chunks
1 potato, cut in chunks
2 carrots, cut in chunks
1 stalk celery, cut in ½-inch pieces
3½ cups V-8® Vegetable Juice
Salt and pepper, to taste
1 tablespoon flour blended with equal amount of water

Rub tripe with baking soda; rinse off. Place tripe in pot; cover with water and parboil tripe about 15 minutes (longer if softer tripe is desired); drain, rinse and slice into bite-size pieces. Place back in pot; add V-8® juice. Bring to boil; add rest of vegetables. Simmer until vegetables are tender. Add salt and pepper, to taste. Add flour mixture to thicken as desired.

☛ NOTE: *Another of Merv Chun's favorite easy recipes. You may add a few drops of Tabasco® sauce for added flavor or a pinch of sugar if you like it a little sweeter.*

Vegetable Meat Loaf

Yield: 8 servings

2 pounds ground beef
2 eggs
½ onion, chopped
1 can vegetable soup (10.5 oz.)
1¼ cup Quick 1-minute oats
¼ cup ketchup
2 teaspoons salt
¼ teaspoon pepper

Mix ingredients thoroughly; press into loaf pan. Bake at 400°, uncovered, for 1 hour.

Hamburger Curry

Yield: 4 servings

1 pound ground beef
1 onion, chopped
1 tablespoon oil
1½ cups water
1 can peas and carrots (14.5 oz.)
1 to 2 tablespoons curry powder (adjust to taste)
½ teaspoon sugar
Salt and pepper, to taste
2 tablespoons flour blended with equal amount water

Heat oil and fry onions until tender. Add ground beef; stir-fry until browned. Add water, peas and carrots, liquid included. Bring to boil; add curry, sugar, and salt and pepper. Lower heat and simmer for a few minutes. Thicken gravy with flour blended with water.

NOTE: *A real local favorite that is quick and easy. Serve over rice.*

Korean Burgers

Yield: 3-4 servings

1 pound ground beef
½ cup kimchee, finely chopped
2 stalks green onion (about ¼ cup), thinly sliced
1 clove garlic, minced
¼ cup flour
½ teaspoon salt
1 tablespoon sugar
2 tablespoons soy sauce
2 teaspoons oil
Flour for coating
1 egg, beaten

Mix first 8 ingredients thoroughly. Shape into small thin patties; set aside. Heat oil in frying pan. Coat each patty with flour, dip in beaten egg and fry until brown on both sides. Add more oil, if needed.

Quick Corned Beef and Cabbage

Yield: 4 servings

1 can corned beef (12 oz.)
1 onion, sliced
1 tablespoon oil
1 small head cabbage, cut in chunks
Salt and pepper, to season
Sugar and soy sauce, to taste (optional)

Heat oil and sauté onion. Add corned beef and cook for about a minute. Add cabbage. (Add a little water for moisture, if necessary.) Cover and cook until cabbage is softened. Season with salt and pepper. Add sugar and soy sauce to taste, if desired.

☛ NOTE: *This is such a classic local dish that is quick and easy. Almost everyone has a can or two of corned beef in his cupboard.*

Kimchee Patties

Yield: 4 servings

1 pound ground beef
1 cup kimchee, chopped and squeezed
1 small onion, chopped
¼ cup green onions, thinly sliced
6 stems watercress, chopped
3 eggs
¼ cup flour
1 teaspoon salt
Black pepper, to taste
1 tablespoon oil for frying

Mix all ingredients (except oil). Heat oil, make patties and fry.

☛ NOTE: *A favorite among young adults.*

Quickie Chop Steak

Yield: 5 to 6 servings

1 pound top round steak, sliced
2 tablespoons flour
½ teaspoon salt
Pepper, to taste
2 tablespoons oil
1 clove garlic, crushed
1 tablespoon soy sauce
1 teaspoon sugar
1 onion, sliced
1 stalk celery, slivered
1 tomato, cut into wedges
1 teaspoon Worcestershire® sauce

Sprinkle meat with flour, salt and pepper. Heat oil in skillet; sauté garlic. Stir-fry meat until half done. Add soy sauce and sugar; stir. Add onion and celery; stir-fry until half done. Add tomato and Worcestershire® sauce; cook until done.

☛ NOTE: *Do not overcook. Vegetables should be just barely done.*

Hamburger and Spinach

Yield: 3 to 4 servings

1 pound ground beef or ground chicken
1 tablespoon oil
1 clove garlic, crushed
Salt and pepper, to taste
1 large bunch spinach (about 1 pound), chopped into 2-inch lengths
Soy sauce, to taste (optional)
3 eggs, beaten

In large skillet, heat oil; brown garlic and ground beef. Season with salt and black pepper. Drain off fat. Add spinach and stir-fry until limp. Add soy sauce to taste, if desired. Add eggs and stir occasionally until cooked.

☛ NOTE: *A wonderful way to serve spinach to your family! To clean spinach, place spinach in large container of water and rinse leaves. Cut off root ends and discard.*

Goulash

Yield: 4 to 6 servings

2 tablespoons oil
½ onion, chopped
1 pound ground beef
2 cans tomato sauce (8 oz. each)
1 box frozen mixed vegetables (10 oz.)
Salt and pepper, to taste

Fry onion in hot oil; add beef. Cook, stirring, until light brown. Stir in tomato sauce and frozen vegetables. Simmer until vegetables are thawed and heated. Season with salt and pepper. Simmer for 5 more minutes.

☛ NOTE: *A great favorite! It's quick and makes a satisfying meal for the children.*

Meatballs

Yield: 12 servings

2 eggs, divided
2 pounds ground beef
1½ cups Italian-style bread crumbs, divided
1 teaspoon salt
¾ teaspoon garlic powder
½ teaspoon black pepper

Place foil on 2 baking sheets with sides and spray generously with non-stick cooking spray; set aside.

Lightly beat one egg in large bowl. Add beef, ½ cup bread crumbs, salt, garlic powder and pepper. Shape about 2 tablespoons beef mixture into roughly 2-inch circles.

Lightly beat remaining egg. Place one cup bread crumbs in another bowl. Dip meatballs in beaten egg; roll in bread crumbs. Place on foil-lined baking sheet; bake at 350° for 35 minutes or until meatballs are slightly crisp, turning meatballs over once.

☛ NOTE: *Recommended by my granddaughter, Kristen, when she made a version of these meatballs with her mother. Everyone liked it. Serve with pasta and spaghetti sauce.*

No-Fail Roast Beef

Yield: 4 to 5 servings

Rib roast beef (about 2 to 3 ribs or more)
Salt and pepper, to taste
2 cloves garlic (optional), cut in small pieces

Salt and pepper roast. (Optional: poke holes here and there in roast and insert little pieces of garlic.) Let stand at room temperature for 1 hour. Place beef, fat side up, in open roaster (uncovered) and put in pre-heated 350° oven for 1 hour. Turn off heat but DO NOT OPEN DOOR AT ANY TIME UNTIL READY TO SERVE.

Allow at least 3 hours or more in oven to complete cooking.

For rare beef: 45 minutes before serving, turn oven on to 300°.
For medium beef: 50 minutes before serving, turn oven on to 300°.
For medium-well done: 55 minutes before serving, turn oven on to 300°.

☛ NOTE: *You won't believe how perfectly your roast will be cooked. Everyone who has tried this recipe has told me it really is No-Fail!*

Ham Steak

Yield: 2 to 3 servings

1 ham steak (1 pound)
¼ cup brown sugar, or more to your taste
1 tablespoon vinegar
1 teaspoon Colman's® mustard

Preheat pan on medium heat. Cook ham steak in hot pan about 2 to 3 minutes per side. Mix rest of ingredients and pour over ham steak. Lower heat and if necessary, cook until liquid is reduced.

☛ NOTE: *Quick and tasty! At our 50th Hilo High School class reunion, Naomi Hayakawa shared this easy and simple dish. She says it's great for breakfast, too.*

Pork

Baked SPAM®

Yield: 4 to 6 servings

2 cans SPAM®, 25% less sodium (12 oz. each)
⅓ cup brown sugar
1 can crushed pineapple (8 oz.)
Whole cloves (about 20)

Lay SPAM® flat in a baking pan. Score SPAM® and stud SPAM® with cloves. Spread brown sugar on top and sides, then cover with pineapple. Bake, uncovered, at 350° for 30 minutes.

☛ NOTE: *It's amazing how popular Baked SPAM® is in Hawai'i. It's the great SPAM® capital! Mineko Hayashi Takeuchi volunteered this recipe as a great quick and easy one at our 50th reunion in Hilo. Everyone agreed it's a winner.*

SPAM® and Cabbage

Yield: 4 servings

1 can SPAM®
1 tablespoon oil
½ onion, cut in slices
½ head cabbage, shredded (about 10 cups)
Salt and pepper, to taste

Cut SPAM® into 9 slices; then cut again into narrow rectangular pieces. Heat oil, stir-fry onion slices until softened. Add SPAM® pieces; stir fry. Add shredded cabbage and cook together until cabbage is softened to your taste. Add salt and pepper, to taste.

☛ NOTE: *This is a rendition of the famous Olaa "8 Mile Half" Camp dish that they laughingly said could serve 22 people in the "old days". Max Calica volunteered this recipe as a fond memory of life in Olaa on the Big Island.*

Easy Ham Casserole

Yield: 5 to 6 servings

1 potato, peeled and sliced
2 cups ham, cubed
1 onion, sliced
1 can whole kernel corn (11 oz.), drained
1 can cut or sliced green beans (14.5 oz.), drained
1 can cream of mushroom soup (10¾ oz.)
½ cup milk

Layer ingredients in order listed in a greased, 2-quart casserole dish. Cover and bake at 350° for 30 minutes.

Bittermelon with Pork

Yield: 6 to 8 servings

3 bittermelon
¾ pound ground pork
1 tablespoon oil
1 bulb garlic (20 to 25 cloves), peeled and sliced
1 block firm tofu (20 oz.), drained
1 package dashi no moto (soup stock)
1 cup chicken broth
1 egg, slightly beaten

Cut bittermelon in half lengthwise, remove seeds and cut in ¼-inch diagonal slices. Set aside.

Heat oil and cook ground pork with garlic. Add tofu; break into bite-size pieces with wooden spoon as it cooks. Add bittermelon and chicken broth. Sprinkle with dashi no moto and continue cooking, stirring occasionally, until bittermelon is still slightly crunchy (about 5 minutes). Mix in egg; cook 1 minute more.

☛ NOTE: *A very popular Okinawan dish! Although the recipe calls for the bittermelon to be crunchy, I prefer mine to be on the softer side.*

Ma Po Tofu

Yield: 2 to 3 servings

¼ pound ground pork
2 tablespoons oil
⅛ cup dried shrimp, soaked and drained
¾ cup chicken broth
1 block firm tofu (20 oz.), cut into 1 x 2-inch cubes
1 stalk green onion, finely cut for garnish

Sauce:
2 tablespoons cornstarch
2 tablespoons water
2 tablespoons soy sauce
1 tablespoon oyster sauce
1 teaspoon salt (or less)
1 teaspoon chili garlic sauce

Heat oil; sauté ground pork and dried shrimp. Add broth; bring to boil. Lower heat and simmer, covered, for 5 minutes. Add tofu and stir lightly until well heated. Add sauce mixture and heat until thickened. Garnish with green onions.

☛ NOTE: *Add more chicken broth if gravy is too thick. In spite of the many ingredients this dish is really quick and easy to prepare. Very tasty served over hot rice!*

Roast Pork

Yield: 6 servings

3 to 4 pounds pork butt (or pork shoulder)
Salt, pepper, and garlic salt, to season

Place pork on foil-lined 9 x 13-inch pan. Season pork with salt, pepper and garlic salt. Place in 350° oven and bake 35 minutes per pound (about 1 hour and 45 minutes to 2 hours and 20 minutes). Slice and serve with your favorite gravy.

Mushroom Pork Chops

Yield: 3 to 4 servings

6 pork chops
Oil for browning
Salt, pepper, garlic salt to season
1 can cream of mushroom soup (10¾ oz.)
1½ cups milk

Season pork chops with salt, pepper and garlic salt. Heat oil and brown pork chops. Place in foil-lined 9 x 13-inch pan. Combine soup with milk; pour mixture over pork chops. Place in 350° oven and bake for 1 hour.

☛ NOTE: *A favorite for the busy family.*

Pork Guisantes

Yield: 4 to 6 servings

1½ pound pork shoulder
3 cloves garlic, minced
1 teaspoon salt
¼ teaspoon pepper
1 can tomato sauce (8 oz.)
1 jar sliced pimientos (2 oz.)
1 package frozen peas (10 oz.)

Slice pork, separating fatty and lean pieces. (Do not discard fat.) Brown pork fat slices with garlic. Add lean pork; cook, stirring occasionally, until liquid evaporates (about 15 to 20 minutes). Add salt, pepper and tomato sauce; simmer 20 minutes, stirring occasionally. Add pimientos and peas; cook until heated.

☛ NOTE: *After browning pork fat slices, if desired, remove from pan and drain fat or use paper towel to remove excess oil.*

Pork Kimchee

Yield: 3 to 4 servings

½ pound lean pork, thinly sliced
2 teaspoons oil
2 to 3 cloves garlic, crushed
1-inch fresh ginger, grated
1 teaspoon soy sauce, or more to taste
½ teaspoon sugar, or more to taste
1 container firm tofu (20 oz.), drained and cubed
1 jar kimchee (e.g., Kohala® Won-Bok Kimchee)

Heat pan and add oil. When oil is hot, sauté garlic and ginger. Add pork; stir-fry, adding soy sauce and sugar. Add tofu; heat thoroughly. Add entire jar of kimchee with liquid. (If desired, begin with ½ jar and then add more to your taste.)

☛ NOTE: *While at Border's in Maui, I met Rene Parabicoli who says her husband thoroughly enjoys this dish. It's easy and tasty! She uses the entire jar of kimchee for best flavor.*

Quickie Pineapple SPAM®

Yield: 5 to 6 servings

2 cans SPAM®, sliced into 16 pieces
½ cup brown sugar
1 can pineapple juice (6 oz.)
1 teaspoon prepared yellow mustard (e.g., French's®)

Place SPAM® slices in 9 x 13-inch pan. Mix brown sugar, pineapple juice and mustard; spread over SPAM®. Bake at 350° for 15 to 20 minutes.

☛ NOTE: *Another easy recipe from the files of Nancy Ueda who generously shared several of her easy-to-cook recipes with me.*

☛ VARIATION: *My sister-in-law, Mimi, says she doesn't even use the oven. She fries the SPAM® slices and then simmers them with brown sugar and pineapple (juice, chunks or crushed).*

Sweet Sour Ribs

Yield: 4 to 5 servings

1½ to 2 pounds ribs (e.g., sweet and sour spareribs)
2 tablespoons cornstarch
2 tablespoons brown sugar
2 tablespoons soy sauce
1 teaspoon salt
1 inch piece fresh ginger, crushed
Oil for browning

Sauce:
3 tablespoons brown sugar
3 tablespoons vinegar
½ cup water

Mix together cornstarch, brown sugar, soy sauce, salt and ginger; add ribs. Coat ribs and let stand 15 minutes. Combine sauce ingredients; set aside.

Pour oil about ¼-inch deep in pot. Heat oil and brown ribs slightly. Remove excess oil. Add sauce to spare ribs and bring to boil. Lower heat and simmer, covered, for 1 hour, or until softened. Stir occasionally.

- NOTE: *"The best!" This was highly recommended by my good friend and neighbor, Evelyn Shiraki. She says she got the recipe from her friend, Rowena, in 1959.*

- VARIATION: *Add sliced carrots, daikon or pineapple chunks, and heat just before serving.*

Side Street Pork Chops

Yield: 2 to 3 servings

4 pork chops, about 1½-inches thick
1 tablespoon garlic salt
2 teaspoons pepper
½ cup flour
⅓ cup cornstarch
1 cup canola oil

Mix together garlic salt, pepper, flour and cornstarch; coat pork chops. Heat oil and fry chops about 10 minutes, turning frequently until browned. Cut meat from bones; slice.

- SUGGESTION: *Serve sliced pork chops over shredded cabbage.*
- NOTE: *Pork chops are tender and very tasty! The original recipe was shared by my neighbor, Evelyn Shiraki, many years ago. We really like this.*
- HINT: *After coating the pork chops let them sit for at least 30 minutes to get rid of the chill and they'll be easier to cook.*

Chicken Paprika

Yield: 3 to 4 servings

5 to 6 chicken thighs, boneless and skinless
Butter
1 teaspoon paprika
1 teaspoon salt
1 teaspoon sugar
¼ teaspoon pepper

Arrange chicken in foil-lined pan and dot with butter. Mix together remaining ingredients and sprinkle over chicken. Bake at 425° for approximately 45 minutes. Check for doneness.

Thai Chicken Curry, page 76

Beef and Snow Peas, page 52

Sweet Sour Ribs, page 65

Buffalo Wings, page 9

Edamame Rice, page 84

Spinach and Feta Pasta Salad, page 28

Broccoli with Sunflower Seeds, page 30

Peach Cake, page 100

Garden Vegetable Soup, page 21

Butterfish with Soy Sauce, page 79

Easy Mint Chocolate Chip Pie, page 115

Oxtail Soup with Red Beans, page 24

Ground Turkey Lettuce Wraps, page 78

Date Nut Bread, page 96

Waffle Treat, page 121

Chicken with Papaya Seed Dressing

Yield: 4 to 5 servings

2 pounds chicken thighs, boneless and skinless

Marinade:
1 bottle Hawaiian Hula® papaya seed dressing (8 oz.)
½ cup soy sauce
½ cup sugar

Combine marinade and marinate chicken overnight. Grill over hibachi or place in foil-lined roasting pan and bake in sauce at 350° for 1 hour.

Barbecue Chicken Thighs

Yield: 4 to 5 servings

4 pounds chicken thighs

Marinade:
½ cup soy sauce
½ cup ketchup
¾ cup sugar
¼ cup sherry
1 clove garlic, grated
1-inch piece fresh ginger, grated
⅓ cup flour

Place chicken, skin side up, in foil-lined 9 x 13-inch pan. Mix marinade ingredients and pour over chicken. Bake, uncovered, at 350° for 1 hour.

☛ NOTE: *Very easy and tasty! While chicken is baking, cook the rice and prepare a green salad.*

Chicken Katsu

Yield: 6 servings

2 pounds chicken breasts, boneless and skinless
Garlic salt to season
½ cup flour
2 eggs, beaten
2 cups Panko flakes (flour meal for breading)
Oil for frying

Katsu Sauce:
⅓ cup ketchup
¼ cup soy sauce
¼ cup sugar
1½ teaspoons Worcestershire® sauce
Pinch ground red pepper

Combine all katsu sauce ingredients; mix well. Set aside.

Season chicken generously with garlic salt and let stand 15 to 30 minutes. Heat about ½ inch oil in skillet. Dredge chicken in flour, dip in eggs, and coat with Panko in that order. Fry chicken until golden brown on both sides; drain on paper towels. Cut into 1-inch slices. Serve with katsu sauce.

☛ NOTE: *Chicken breasts should not be too thick; cut in half horizontally or pound chicken to flatten. To make this dish even easier, use a prepared katsu sauce of your choice (e.g., Kikkoman Tonkatsu sauce.)*

Easy Roast Chicken

Yield: 2 to 3 servings

2 to 3 pounds fryer
Hawaiian salt, to season
1 clove garlic, grated

Rinse fryer and pat dry. Rub Hawaiian salt (and garlic, if desired) in cavity and all over chicken. Place in pan or corningware. Bake at 400° for 1 hour.

☛ NOTE: *After rubbing salt over chicken, chicken may be refrigerated overnight and cooked the next day. Thanks to Lorna Tam Ho for sharing this very easy and very delicious recipe!*

Chicken Long Rice

Yield: 6 to 8 servings

2 pounds chicken thighs, skinless and boneless
2 tablespoons oil
1 clove garlic, crushed
1-inch piece fresh ginger, crushed
1 onion, sliced
2 cans chicken broth (14.5 oz. each)
2 bundles long rice (2 oz. each), soaked in hot water
Pepper, to season
1 stalk green onion, cut in 2-inch lengths

Cut chicken into bite size pieces (about 1½-inch pieces). Sauté garlic and ginger in oil. Add onion and chicken and fry until slightly browned. Add chicken broth; bring to boil. Skim off fat and "scum." Lower heat and simmer for 40 minutes.

Cut soaked long rice into 3 to 4-inch lengths. Add long rice, pepper and green onion to chicken simmering in broth and cook 10 minutes longer.

☛ NOTE: *Another local favorite!*

Chicken Tofu

Yield: 4 servings

½ to 1 pound chicken breast, thinly sliced
1½ tablespoons oil
2½ tablespoons sugar
1 tablespoon mirin
⅓ cup soy sauce
2 thin slices fresh ginger, crushed
1 small round onion, thinly sliced
1 medium carrot, julienned
3 stalks green onion, cut in 1-inch lengths (about ½ cup)
1 block tofu, cut in 1-inch cubes

Heat oil; add chicken and stir-fry. Add sugar, mirin, soy sauce and ginger; cook 2 minutes. Add round onion, carrots and green onion; cook additional minute. Add tofu; cook until tofu is heated through.

Easy Curry for Two

Yield: 2 servings

2 chicken thighs, boneless and skinless, cut into bite-size pieces
1 can cream of mushroom soup (10¾ oz.)
2 tablespoons water
Curry mix pieces (e.g., S&B® Golden Curry)

Heat cream of mushroom soup with 2 tablespoons water. Break off a small piece from the curry mix and blend with soup. Taste and add more pieces as desired. Heat to boiling, add chicken and simmer for about 15 to 20 minutes or until chicken is tender and done.

- NOTE: *Select mild, medium or hot curry. Many brands are available.*

- VARIATION: *Substitute chicken with shrimp. Add frozen or canned vegetables.*

Minute Chicken

Yield: 4 to 5 servings

1½ pounds chicken thighs, boneless and skinless
1½ tablespoons flour
2 tablespoon oil
1 clove garlic, crushed

Seasoning:
1 tablespoon sugar
¼ teaspoon pepper
⅓ cup oyster sauce
⅓ cup water
½ cup green onion, chopped

Cut chicken into bite-sized pieces. Dredge in flour; let stand 10 minutes. Heat oil; add garlic and chicken. Stir-fry until chicken is brown. Reduce heat; add seasoning.

☛ NOTE: *My sister-in-law, Mimi Hee, volunteered this very quick and easy tasty meal. Serve with hot rice.*

Stuffed Chicken

Yield: 4 servings

4 pieces skinless, boneless chicken breasts
1 box frozen spinach (10 oz.), thawed and drained
4 slices white cheese (e.g., Swiss)
4 slices ham (sandwich type)
1 can cream of mushroom (or celery) soup (10¾ oz.)

Lightly pound chicken to flatten. Place chicken right side down on flat surface. Top with slice of ham, cheese and spinach. (Squeeze spinach to remove excess liquid.) Roll and secure with toothpicks. Place in microwave-safe container. Pour condensed soup over chicken bundles. Cover with plastic wrap. Microwave on HIGH for 15 to 25 minutes.

☛ NOTE: *Another way to add spinach to a meal in a very tasty style.*

Chicken Stir-Fry

Yield: 2 to 3 servings

2 to 4 chicken thighs, boneless and skinless, cut into thin slices
Fresh ginger slice (optional)
1 clove garlic, crushed (optional)
1 pound vegetable of your choice (e.g., green beans, asparagus, Chinese cabbage, mixed vegetables, etc.)

Marinade:
2 tablespoons soy sauce
1 tablespoon cornstarch
1 tablespoon sherry
½ teaspoon sugar
Dash sesame oil

Mix together marinade; marinate chicken for 30 minutes or longer.

Heat about 1 to 2 tablespoons oil in nonstick frying pan and stir-fry vegetables; sprinkle with salt, to season. Do not overcook. Remove from pan. Add 1 tablespoon more oil to the same pan and heat. Add fresh ginger slice and 1 clove garlic, if desired; then stir-fry marinated chicken until just done. Add back vegetables and quickly stir-fry.

☛ NOTE: *Marinated chicken may be prepared earlier, refrigerated or frozen for later use. What's great is that you can use any type of vegetables you may have in your vegetable bin to create a quick meal. A nonstick frying pan is highly recommended.*

Fried Chicken

Yield: 3 to 4 servings

3 pounds chicken parts
1 tablespoon Hawaiian salt
1 egg, beaten
½ teaspoon salt
Oil for frying, 1-inch deep

Flour Mixture:
2 cups cornstarch
½ cup flour
1 tablespoon garlic salt
1 teaspoon pepper

Rub Hawaiian salt all over chicken and let set for 30 minutes.

Preheat oil in large heavy skillet on medium high heat (350°).

Combine flour mixture in a plastic bag. Mix egg and ½ teaspoon salt together. Dip chicken in egg. Place in flour mixture and shake well until coated. Place chicken skin side down in frying pan. Turn over when brown. Test for doneness before removing from oil. Drain on paper towel.

Shoyu Chicken

Yield: 3 to 4 servings

6 chicken thighs, with bone and skin
½ cup sugar
½ cup soy sauce
1 clove garlic, grated (optional)
1-inch piece ginger, grated (optional)

Place all ingredients in pot; bring to boil. Lower heat, cover and simmer for about 35 to 45 minutes.

☛ NOTE: *Ono! A real local favorite! Serve with hot rice, corn and a vegetable salad for a satisfying local dinner. Chicken may be simmered longer, if desired.*

Baked Cantonese Chicken

Yield: 3 servings

3 pounds chicken thighs

Marinade:
¼ cup soy sauce
¼ cup lemon juice (about 2 lemons)
¼ cup honey
½ cup ketchup
1 tablespoon sherry
1 small piece ginger, crushed

Combine marinade ingredients and marinate chicken overnight in refrigerator. When ready to cook, place chicken in foil-lined baking pan. Pour remaining sauce over chicken. Bake at 350° for 50 minutes or until chicken is done.

Miso Chicken

Yield: 2 servings

4 chicken thighs
2 tablespoons oil

Sauce:
2 tablespoons sugar
2 tablespoons red miso
3 tablespoons sake
1 tablespoon mirin
2 tablespoons soup stock (e.g., Hon-Dashi Bonito Fish Soup Stock)

Mix together sauce ingredients; set aside.

Heat oil; fry chicken until browned. Pour sauce over chicken. Simmer, covered, for 30 to 45 minutes, turning chicken over occasionally.

☛ NOTE: *Great miso flavor.*

Moist Baked Chicken

Yield: 4 to 6 servings

2 to 3 pounds chicken thighs, with bone and skin
1 package Good Seasons® Zesty Italian Salad Dressing mix (0.6 oz.)
½ cup mayonnaise
Bread crumbs for coating (e.g., Progresso® Italian Style Bread Crumbs)

Combine dressing mix and mayonnaise; mix well. Rinse and pat dry chicken; coat chicken with mayonnaise mixture. Roll in bread crumbs. Place in foil-lined pan and bake at 350° for 45 to 60 minutes.

☛ NOTE: *Very moist and full of flavor!*

Thai Chicken Curry

Yield: 2 to 3 servings

2 small chicken breasts, cut into small pieces
½ cup coconut milk
½ cup chicken broth
1 teaspoon green curry paste (e.g., Mae Ploy®)
1 tablespoon soy sauce
1 teaspoon brown sugar
1 tablespoon fish sauce (e.g., UFC Nguyen Chat Nuoc Mam)
1 cup frozen peas
½ teaspoon salt (more or less to taste)
¼ teaspoon pepper (more or less to taste)
2 teaspoons cornstarch blended with 2 teaspoons water
Fresh Thai basil leaves

Heat saucepan. Add chicken broth, coconut milk and curry paste. Stir and cook until heated through. Add chicken, soy sauce and sugar; simmer 5 to 10 minutes or more. Add fish sauce and peas. Season with salt and pepper. Thicken with blended cornstarch. Add desired amount of basil leaves into curry. Heat thoroughly and serve. Garnish with basil leaves, if desired.

- NOTE: *Add more broth and coconut milk if necessary. Catherine Seah made this dish and she also prepared Jasmine rice to go with it for a church potluck dinner. So delicious! I loved it and had to ask her for the recipe. She told me this is so easy to prepare and it is. The list of ingredients is rather long but it is quick and easy. Recipe may be easily doubled.*

- VARIATION: *Add 1 yellow or orange bell pepper, thinly sliced, same time as basil leaves.*

Tarragon Chicken

Yield: 4 to 5 servings

2 pounds chicken drumsticks or boned breasts
Salt and pepper, to taste
2 tablespoons butter
½ onion, sliced
½ cup white wine
1 container white mushrooms (8 oz.), sliced
⅛ teaspoon tarragon
½ cup evaporated milk (or heavy cream)

Salt and pepper chicken; brown in melted butter. Add onions; cook until translucent. Add wine, mushrooms and tarragon. Simmer, covered, for 20 to 30 minutes or until chicken is cooked. Add cream to make sauce. Adjust to taste.

☛ NOTE: *Love this! Smells great and tastes great.*

Turkey Divan

2 to 3 servings

1 crown broccoli, chopped into bite-size pieces
2 cups shredded cooked turkey
1 can cream of mushroom soup (10¾ oz.)

Place broccoli in a casserole dish and cook in microwave (until slightly undercooked). Place shredded turkey over broccoli. Pour cream of mushroom soup over turkey and cook in microwave, about 4 minutes on high. Mix before serving.

☛ VARIATION: *Substitute turkey with huli huli chicken.*

☛ NOTE: *Great for left-over turkey! My cousin, Judy Takabayashi, suggested this "quick and easy" recipe; it's one of her favorites.*

Turkey Patties

Yield: 6 servings

1½ pounds frozen ground turkey, thawed
1 small onion, minced
3 tablespoons flour
½ cup milk
1 egg
½ teaspoon salt
½ teaspoon pepper
Olive oil for frying

Thaw ground turkey, drain well. Place in large bowl (check for any more liquid still draining out). Add remaining ingredients, except olive oil, and mix together. Let rest 30 minutes. Form into patties. Heat olive oil and fry patties until browned on both sides.

☛ NOTE: *If desired, cook onions separately until soft; cool and mix together with rest of ingredients.*

Ground Turkey Lettuce Wraps

Yield: 9 to 10 servings

1 tablespoon oil
½ pound ground turkey
½ can SPAM®, chopped
12 water chestnuts, chopped
1 tablespoon plum sauce
1 tablespoon hoisin sauce
Lettuce leaves

Heat oil; add turkey. Break apart ground turkey into small pieces while cooking. When turkey is done, add SPAM®; cook 5 minutes. Add water chestnuts, plum sauce and hoisin sauce. Stir-fry 5 minutes. Fill lettuce leaves; wrap and serve.

Butterfish

Yield: 2 to 3 servings

1 pound frozen butterfish steaks (about 2 pieces)
Salt and pepper, to taste
Panko flakes for coating
Non-stick cooking spray to coat frying pan

Salt and pepper butterfish. Coat with Panko flakes. Spray cooking spray on fry pan; heat and fry fish on medium to medium-low until browned on both sides. Check for doneness.

Butterfish with Soy Sauce

Yield: 3 to 4 servings

1 pound butterfish
Salt and pepper, to season
Flour for dredging
1 to 2 tablespoons oil

Sauce:
¼ cup soy sauce
5 tablespoons sugar
1 stalk green onion, chopped
1 large clove garlic, minced
Chili pepper or crushed red pepper, to season (optional)

Combine sauce ingredients and mix well.

Salt and pepper butterfish. Dredge in flour and fry. When fish is done, pour sauce over. Serve or simmer in sauce for a few minutes before serving.

☛ NOTE: *My daughter, Jennifer, loves this. A real local favorite! Another of my mom's recipes which she passed on to me.*

Chinese Steamed Fish

Yield: 3 to 4 servings

3 pounds whole fish (with head and tail on), cleaned
Soy sauce, to season
½ cup green onion, finely chopped
¼ cup fresh ginger, finely chopped
¼ cup chung choi, finely chopped
1 cup peanut oil, heated

Pour small amount of soy sauce in cavity of fish. Steam fish for 20 to 25 minutes. When fish is cooked, remove and place on a platter. Mix together green onion, ginger and chung choi and place over fish. Pour hot sizzling peanut oil over chopped ingredients and fish. Serve immediately.

☛ NOTE: *If elongated fish steamer pan is unavailable, cut fish into large pieces to fit in a dish that will fit in a round-type steamer.*

Chinese Style Shrimp

Yield: 3 servings

1 pound shrimp (21-25 size), unshelled
¼ cup cornstarch for coating
2 tablespoons oil
½ teaspoon Hawaiian salt
1 inch fresh ginger, minced
1 clove garlic, minced
1 teaspoon oyster sauce, more or less to taste
¼ cup sherry
1 tablespoon green onions, chopped

Roll unshelled shrimp in cornstarch to coat; set aside. Heat oil and salt; sauté ginger and garlic on medium heat. Add shrimp, and when almost done, add oyster sauce to taste. Add sherry. Garnish with chopped green onions.

Salmon with Tokyo Zuke

Yield: 4 to 6 servings

1½ to 2 pounds salmon fillet
1 can Fukujinzuke "seasoned vegetables" (Tokyo Zuke), (7.76 oz.)

Cut salmon into serving pieces. Place salmon on foil in pan. Spread 1 can Tokyo Zuke over salmon. Cover pan with another piece of foil and seal. Bake in oven at 350° for 30 to 35 minutes or until done.

- NOTE: *My friend, Nancy Ueda, shared this unusual but tasty salmon as one of her easy recipes.*

Furikake Salmon

Yield: 2 servings

1 salmon fillet, cut in portion sizes
Mayonnaise
Furikake (e.g., Aji Nori Furikake)
1 tablespoon butter

Generously spread mayonnaise on one side of salmon. Sprinkle furikake generously over mayonnaise. Heat pan on medium heat and add butter. Place salmon furikake-side down. Lower heat to medium-low and slowly cook for 10 to 15 minutes. While cooking, spread mayonnaise and furikake on top. Turn over and cook other side.

- OPTIONAL: *If desired, serve cooked salmon with the following sauce.*

Sauce:

2 tablespoons butter
2 cloves garlic, minced
¼ cup soy sauce
2 tablespoons sugar

Melt butter. Add garlic and stir. Blend in soy sauce and sugar and simmer for 1 to 2 minutes. Pour over cooked salmon.

Wiki-Wiki Creamed Tuna

Yield: 3 servings

1 can cream of mushroom soup (10¾ oz.)
½ can water (use mushroom soup can)
1 can tuna (6 oz.), drained
½ cup frozen or canned peas, carrots or corn
Salt and pepper to taste (optional)

Place mushroom soup and ½ can water into small saucepan; mix together. Add tuna; simmer on low heat until heated through, stirring occasionally. Add vegetables just before serving. Season with salt and pepper, if desired.

☛ NOTE: *Tastes great over hot rice!*

Linguine with White Clam Sauce

Yield: 5 to 6 servings

½ cup butter (1 stick)
¼ cup olive oil
6 to 8 cloves garlic, minced or pressed
3 cans chopped clams (6½ oz. each), DO NOT DRAIN
1 cup parsley flakes
1 teaspoon oregano
1 teaspoon basil
½ teaspoon crushed red pepper
1 package linguine (16 oz.), cooked according to package instructions

Melt butter in olive oil. Add garlic; cook until golden. (Do not burn garlic.) Add clams with liquid and rest of ingredients. Simmer for 5 minutes. Toss mixture with cooked linguine.

☛ NOTE: *Very tasty. For best results, toss clam sauce with linguine immediately after linguine is cooked and drained. Do not rinse with water.*

☛ SUGGESTION: *If you like more clams, add another can of chopped clams, drained, to sauce.*

Chorizo Rice

Yield: 12-14 servings

3 cups long grain rice (e.g., Jasmine Rice)
½ onion, chopped
2 teaspoons oil
1 beef chorizo sausage (12 oz.), casing removed and coarsely chopped
1 bunch Chinese parsley, cut in 1-inch lengths (optional)
1 can black beans (15.5 oz.), drained

Rinse rice, drain and add 3 cups water. Cook rice; set aside. Heat oil in non-stick frying pan; add onions and cook until softened. Add chorizo; stir-fry. Add Chinese parsley, if desired, and mix together. Turn off heat. Add hot cooked rice and beans; gently and thoroughly mix together. Salt and pepper to taste.

☛ NOTE: *Merv Chun came up with this tasty concoction when he bought some chorizo one day and discovered that it fell apart when he removed the casing. He added rice and beans and "accidentally" created chorizo rice. This dish is so easy to prepare. Great for a potluck.*

Broiled Sushi

Yield: 35-40 servings

3 cups rice (or 4 rice cooker "cups"), cooked
1 pound imitation crab, shredded
1 cup sour cream (8 oz.)
1 cup mayonnaise
1 to 2 containers tobiko (.13 lb. each), optional
½ bottle furikake (e.g., Nori Komi Furikake)
Korean seasoned seaweed for sushi

Combine imitation crab, sour cream and mayonnaise; set aside. Layer ingredients in 9 x 13-inch pan in the following order: cooked rice, tobiko, furikake, and imitation crab mixture. Broil in oven until top turns brown (about 5-10 minutes). Serve with Korean seasoned seaweed.

Edamame Rice

Yield: 15 to 18 servings

3 cups rice (or 4 rice cooker "cups")
1 package shelled frozen edamame beans (16 oz.), cooked according to package instructions and drained
1 bottle Nametake Seasoned Mushrooms (7.05 oz.), include liquid
1 jar Ochazuke Wakame furikake (1.76 oz.), for sprinkling

Rinse rice; cook in rice cooker. When done, scoop hot rice into large mixing bowl. Add seasoned mushrooms, including liquid, and mix together. Add edamame and toss together gently until mixed together. Top with amount of furikake seasoning desired (about ¼ to ½ jar).

☛ NOTE: *I first tasted this in Hilo at an Amauulu picnic about 10 years ago. My cousin, Miye Watanabe, made it for the potluck gathering. It's still very popular today. Tasted it recently at a Maui tennis luncheon potluck in Wailuku.*

Sticky Rice

Yield: 4 to 5 servings

¼ cup dried shrimp
¼ cup warm water
2 cups mochi (sweet) rice, rinsed and drained
1 can chicken broth (14 oz.)
⅔ cup lup chong, thinly sliced (about 2 pieces)

Soak shrimp in ¼ cup warm water until softened (about 15 minutes). Keep water and chop shrimp. Place shrimp, shrimp water, chicken broth, lup chong and rice into rice cooker. Cook in rice cooker. When done, gently mix together.

☛ NOTE: *I love this! Thanks to my cousin, Judy Kodani Takabayashi, who thought of me and asked her daughter, Robyn, to be sure to give the recipe to me.*

Mushroom Rice

Yield: 8 servings

2 cups rice, rinsed and placed in rice cooker, DO NOT ADD WATER
1 can chicken broth (13¾ oz.)
1 can pieces and stems mushrooms (4 oz.), DO NOT DRAIN
½ teaspoon salt
1 tablespoon soy sauce
2 cups frozen "petite peas" (not necessary to thaw)

Add all ingredients into rice cooker. Turn rice cooker on. When rice is done, mix rice gently before serving.

SPAM® Musubi

Yield: 10 pieces

2½ cups rice (or use 3 rice cooker measuring cups)
1 can SPAM® (12 oz.), cut into 10 slices
10 half sheets nori, 4 x 7-inches each
Acrylic musubi mold

Rinse and cook rice. (Optional: add 1 teaspoon salt to rice for more flavor.) Fry SPAM® slices on both sides. Set aside.

Place mold frame on center of rough side of half sheet nori. Place cooked rice loosely halfway into mold. Place a slice of SPAM® over rice and press firmly with mold press. Remove mold press and frame. Fold nori over rice and SPAM®. Place musubi, overlapping nori side down on plate. Wrap with waxed paper or plastic wrap.

☛ VARIATION: *Teri-SPAM® Musubi*

2 tablespoons sugar
2 tablespoons soy sauce
1 tablespoon mirin

Heat sugar, soy sauce and mirin and cook SPAM® in sauce before making musubi.

Mazegohan

Yield: 6 to 8 servings

2½ cups rice
½ pound gobo root (about 1½ cups), scraped, slivered and soaked in water
2 tablespoons oil
1 container white mushrooms (8 oz.), cut into slivers
1 tablespoon soy sauce, or more to taste
1 round-type red and white kamaboko, "Uzumaki" (6.05 oz.), cut in circles, then into slivers
1 package gobo maki (6.05 oz.), cut into slices
Salt to taste

Rinse and cook rice. (Use slightly less water for drier rice.) While rice is cooking, prepare rest of ingredients.

Heat oil in pan; drain and fry gobo until tender (about 5 minutes). Add mushrooms; stir-fry until softened. Add soy sauce; mix together. Add uzumaki and gobo maki. Cook until heated thoroughly. Set aside.

Scoop hot cooked rice into large mixing bowl. Lightly sprinkle salt over rice and toss gently. Add rest of ingredients and mix together.

Refrigerate any left over mazegohan.

☛ NOTE: *Nancy Fukushima shares this very popular longtime favorite recipe which she learned how to prepare from her mother, Yasuko Ono. In spite of all the directions written, this mazegohan is very easy to prepare. I love the taste of the gobo and mushrooms in this simple dish.*

Tuna Tofu Patties

Yield: 4 servings

1 block firm tofu (20 oz.), drained
1 can tuna (6 oz.), drained
1 egg
¼ cup carrot, grated
¼ cup green onions, chopped
½ to 1 teaspoon salt
1 teaspoon fresh ginger, grated
Pepper, to taste
Oil for frying

Mash tofu with fork. Add all other ingredients and mix well. Place tofu mixture in paper towel-lined sieve and drain for 15 minutes. Shape into 2-inch diameter patties. Fry patties in small amount of oil until brown and firm.

- SUGGESTION: *Serve on bed of shredded lettuce.*
- NOTE: *Very tasty and healthy! Contributed by Ruby Saito who is always looking for light and healthy recipes.*

Tofu Sandwiches

Yield: 5 sandwiches

1 firm tofu (20 oz.), cut into 5 slabs horizontally, drained
1 tablespoon oil
1 onion, sliced
Soy sauce, to taste
1 cucumber, sliced
Iceberg lettuce leaves
Mayonnaise, to taste
Spicy brown mustard, to taste
10 bread slices

Heat oil in non-stick frying pan on medium heat. Use paper towel to absorb water from tofu; fry until both sides are browned. Add onion; sprinkle soy sauce over tofu and onion slices. Continue cooking until onions are translucent. Stir occasionally and check tofu to prevent sticking to pan.

Spread desired amount of mayonnaise and brown mustard on bread slices. Place lettuce leaf on bread, then tofu, onions and cucumber slices. Top with second slice of bread.

- NOTE: *You must try this. So delicious! This is my nephew, Allan Watanabe's favorite lunch sandwich. Ava Olson made it for me, and I was hooked. Very easy to adjust number of sandwiches. Sandwiches can also be refrigerated and eaten later.*

- VARIATION: *For added flavor, sprinkle some nutritional yeast and/or some shredded cheddar cheese over cooked tofu.*

Vienna Sausages and Potatoes

Yield: 2 servings

2 cans Vienna sausages (5 oz. each), cut in half lengthwise
½ onion, sliced
1 large russet potato, sliced in ¼-inch rounds
Salt and pepper, to taste
¾ cup milk

In 8-inch skillet, place layers of sausages, onion and potatoes in that order. Sprinkle salt and pepper over potato slices. Add second layer. Pour milk over. Bring to boil, then lower heat; simmer for 20 to 25 minutes or until potatoes are cooked and soft.

☛ NOTE: *This is such an old-time local favorite which is surprisingly very tasty! Brings back fond memories of my Aunty Kiyoko Kodani who first made it for us many years ago.*

Special Vienna Sausages

Yield: 2 to 3 servings

2 cans Vienna sausages (5 oz. each)
2 teaspoons soy sauce
1 tablespoon sugar (or less to taste)
¼ teaspoon fresh ginger, grated
1 clove garlic, grated
1 teaspoon sake or mirin

Mix together soy sauce, sugar, ginger, garlic and sake; set aside. Place 1 can Vienna sausages, including liquid, in small frying pan. Drain second can and add sausages only to pan. Pour soy sauce mixture over and cook on medium heat, stirring occasionally until sauce is thickened.

☛ NOTE: *For Vienna sausage lovers in Hawai'i! How about Vienna sausages, eggs and rice for breakfast? Yummy!*

Desserts

7-Up® Cake

Yield: 24 to 30 servings

1½ cups butter (3 sticks), softened at room temperature
2½ cups sugar
5 eggs
3 cups flour
2 teaspoons lemon extract
¾ cup 7-Up®

Beat together butter and sugar until frothy and creamy. Add eggs gradually; beat well. Add lemon extract and 7-Up®; beat well. Add flour in 3 to 4 parts; beat well. Pour into greased 9 x 13-inch pan and bake at 325° for 50 to 60 minutes. Check for doneness with skewer.

☛ NOTE: *I really like this cake! It's a little dense, like a pound cake but I enjoyed it without any frosting.*

Banana Bread

Yield: 6 baby loaf pans

4 eggs
1 cup oil
2½ cups flour
1½ cups sugar
2 teaspoons baking powder
2 teaspoons baking soda
1 teaspoon salt
3 cups mashed bananas (about 5 to 6 ripe bananas)
1 teaspoon lemon juice

Beat eggs and add oil. Sift dry ingredients together; add to egg mixture and blend well. Add lemon juice to banana and add to mixture; mix together. Pour into greased baby loaf pans (5¾ x 3¼ x 2) and bake at 350° for 35 to 40 minutes.

☛ NOTE: *For two 9 x 5-inch loaf pans, bake at 350° for 55 minutes or until done.*

Booze Cake

Yield: 24 servings

1 box yellow cake mix (18.25 oz.)
1 box instant French vanilla pudding (3.4 oz.)
1 teaspoon baking powder
4 eggs
½ cup oil
¾ cup water
¼ cup wine or whiskey

Combine all ingredients; mix with electric mixer 2 to 3 minutes. Pour into greased and floured 9 x 13-inch pan. Bake at 350° for 35 to 40 minutes. Sprinkle with powdered sugar when cool.

☛ NOTE: *No taste of any booze! Cake is very moist and not too sweet.*

Black Forest Cake

Yield: about 20 servings

1 box devil's food cake mix (18.25 oz.)
1 cup canola oil
4 eggs
1 can cherry pie filling (21 oz.)

Grease Bundt cake pan. Mix cake mix, oil and eggs for 2 minutes. Fold in pie filling. Pour batter into Bundt cake pan and bake at 350° for 55 minutes. When cool enough to handle, loosen sides gently with butter knife and invert on platter.

☛ NOTE: *Moist and delicious! What a great-tasting cake!*

Carrot Cake

Yield: 24 to 30 servings

2 cups flour
2 cups sugar
2 teaspoons baking soda
1 teaspoon salt
1 teaspoon cinnamon
4 eggs
1¼ cups oil
1 cup nuts, chopped
3 jars baby food carrots, (2.5 oz. each)

Mix all ingredients (adding carrots last). Pour into 9 x 13-inch pan and bake at 350° for 45 minutes.

☛ NOTE: *Tasty but needs a frosting. A frosting suggestion follows, if desired.*

Cream Cheese Frosting:

3 oz. cream cheese, softened
¼ cup butter (half stick), softened
1 tablespoon milk
1 teaspoon vanilla
1¾ cups powdered sugar

Beat together cream cheese, butter, milk and vanilla in small bowl until smooth. Gradually add powdered sugar, beating until smooth.

Butter Pound Cake

Yield: 2 loaf pans

1 box Duncan Hines® butter cake mix (18.25 oz.)
1 container sour cream (8 oz.)
½ cup butter, melted (1 stick)
¼ cup sugar
¼ cup oil
1 teaspoon vanilla
4 eggs

Mix all ingredients; pour into two 9 x 5-inch greased loaf pans. Bake at 325° for 45 minutes, or until wooden skewer inserted in middle comes out clean.

☛ NOTE: *For small baby loaf pans, bake for 35 minutes.*

Choco-Coffee Cake

Yield: 24 servings

1 box devil's food cake mix (18.25 oz.)
¼ cup sugar
4 eggs
½ cup butter (1 stick), melted
⅓ cup oil
⅓ cup water
1 container sour cream (8 oz.)
2 tablespoons plus 1 teaspoon instant coffee crystals
Powdered sugar, for sprinkling

Combine all ingredients (except coffee crystals); beat together 2 to 3 minutes. Fold in coffee crystals. Pour into greased and floured 9 x 13-inch pan. Bake at 350° for 40 to 45 minutes, or until done. Cool.

☛ NOTE: *Dust with powdered sugar or frost with "Cocoa Buttercream Frosting" on page 108.*

Cornmeal Cake

Yield: 16 servings

2 cups Bisquick®
¾ cup sugar
4 tablespoons cornmeal
2 large eggs
1 cup milk
¾ cup butter (1½ sticks), melted

Combine Bisquick®, sugar and cornmeal in large bowl. In smaller bowl, mix together eggs, milk and melted butter with whisk. Put wet mixture into the larger bowl of dry ingredients. Mix together with large spoon and place in 8 x 8-inch pan. Bake at 350° for about 25 to 30 minutes.

☛ NOTE: *Really easy and delicious! May be served warm.*

Dump Cake

Yield: 24 servings

1 can sliced peaches (15 oz.), DO NOT DRAIN
2 cans crushed pineapple (8 oz. each), DO NOT DRAIN
1 box yellow cake mix (18.25 oz.)
½ cup butter or margarine (1 stick), melted

Pour peaches with liquid into 9 x 13-inch pan; cut peaches into smaller pieces. Spread evenly in pan. Spoon pineapple evenly over. Sprinkle cake mix over peaches and pineapple. Spoon melted butter over cake mix. Bake at 300° for 1 hour or until crust is brown.

☛ NOTE: *Serve with vanilla ice cream, if desired. Delicious!*

☛ VARIATION: *Substitute peaches and pineapple with 2 cans Lite Fruit Cocktail (15 of each), do not drain. So quick and easy. Marjorie Maneki Determan shared this version of her husband, Joe's, favorite dessert. He even bakes it himself.*

Date Nut Bread

Yield: 10 servings

1 cup pitted dates, cut up in pieces
1 cup hot water, divided
½ teaspoon baking soda
¾ cup sugar
1 tablespoon butter
1 egg
1½ cups flour
½ teaspoon salt
½ cup walnuts, chopped (optional)

Use ½ cup of the hot water and dissolve baking soda; pour over dates. Set aside to cool.

In bowl, pour remaining ½ cup hot water; add sugar, butter and egg. Mix together. Mix in cooled dates and water. Add flour and salt; mix together. Add walnuts, if desired. Pour in greased loaf pan (Pyrex® or metal) and bake at 350° for 45 to 60 minutes.

☛ NOTE: *Gloria Huber contributed this great recipe that she's had for years. It has a firm texture and is more bread-like. Gloria suggests toasting a slice for breakfast and spreading butter or cream cheese on it. It's great with a cup of coffee.*

Pineapple Angel Food Cake

Yield: 24 servings

1 box Betty Crocker® angel food cake mix (16 oz.)
1 can crushed pineapple in pineapple juice (20 oz.), DO NOT DRAIN

Mix together blending well about 2 minutes. Pour into ungreased 9 x 13-inch pan. Bake at 350° for about 35 to 40 minutes. Check for doneness.

☛ NOTE: *Very light and airy. This is a very simple cake with a strong pineapple flavor. Suggested by Jean Machida Bart as an easy recipe.*

Dobash Cake

Yield: 24 servings

1 box devil's food cake mix (18.25 oz.)
3 eggs
½ cup oil
1 can 7-Up®

Mix all ingredients and bake in greased 9 x 13-inch pan at 350° for 35 to 40 minutes. Cool before frosting.

Frosting:
1½ cups water
1 cup sugar
¼ cup butter (½ stick)
¼ teaspoon salt
⅓ cup cornstarch
½ cup Nestlé's® Nesquick® Chocolate Flavor
½ cup water

Boil together 1½ cups water, sugar, butter and salt. Combine cornstarch, Nesquick® and ½ cup water; add to boiling mixture. Cook until it thickens, stirring constantly. Cool completely before frosting cake. Refrigerate any leftover cake.

☛ NOTE: *Delicious! Easy to make. Cake is light and moist. After refrigeration, cake still tastes great the next day.*

Easy Apple Coffee Cake

Yield: 24 servings

1 can apple pie filling (21 oz.)
3 eggs
1 box yellow cake mix (18.5 oz.)
1 cup walnuts, chopped
⅓ cup brown sugar
1 tablespoon flour
1 teaspoon cinnamon

Butter or grease jelly roll pan. Beat pie filling with eggs in large bowl. Stir in cake mix; beat well. Turn batter into greased pan, spreading evenly. Top with nuts. Combine remaining ingredients in small bowl and mix well. Sprinkle desired amount of brown sugar mixture over nuts. Bake at 350° for 30 to 35 minutes. Cut into squares; serve warm.

☛ NOTE: *This coffee cake is moist and delicious. It tastes best when it is still warm from the oven. I once used blueberry pie filling instead of the apple pie filling and that was also very good.*

Miniature Cream Cheesecakes

Yield: 24 little cakes

2 packages cream cheese (8 oz. each)
¾ cup sugar
1 teaspoon vanilla
2 eggs
1 can cherry or blueberry filling (21 oz.)
1 box vanilla wafers (11 oz.)

Combine cream cheese, sugar, vanilla and eggs. Beat with electric mixer until blended. Place 1 wafer, flat side down, in each cupcake liner in muffin tin. Fill with about 1 tablespoonful of mixture. Bake at 350° for 15 minutes. Cool. Top with pie filling. Refrigerate.

Fresh Apple Cake

Yield: 24 to 30 servings

2 to 3 apples, chopped with skin on (about 4 to 5 cups)
1¾ cups sugar
½ cup oil
2 eggs, well beaten
2 teaspoons vanilla
2 cups flour
2 teaspoons cinnamon
2 teaspoons baking soda
½ teaspoon salt
1 cup nuts, chopped (optional)

Mix apples, sugar and oil; let stand 10 minutes. Add eggs and vanilla; mix well. Sift dry ingredients together; fold into apple mixture. Mix well. Stir in nuts, if desired. Pour into greased 9 x 13-inch pan. Bake at 350° for 1 hour.

☛ NOTE: *Use any type of apple or any combination. This is a great dessert that is not too sweet.*

Sour Cream Chocolate Cake

Yield: about 20 servings

1 box chocolate cake mix (or devil's food cake mix) (18.25 oz.)
1 box instant vanilla pudding (or chocolate pudding mix) (3.5 oz.)
4 eggs
¾ cup oil
1 pint sour cream (2 cups)

Combine cake mix and instant pudding in large bowl. In separate bowl, beat eggs; add oil and sour cream and beat well. Add to cake mixture and mix thoroughly. Pour into greased and floured Bundt pan. Bake at 350° for 45 to 60 minutes.

☛ VARIATION: *Add ½ cup chocolate chips just before pouring batter into pan.*

Peach Cake

Yield: 24 servings

1 box yellow cake mix (18.25 oz.)
1 box instant vanilla pudding (3 oz.)
4 eggs
½ cup oil
1 cup water

Combine all ingredients; beat together 2 to 3 minutes. Place in greased and floured 9 x 13 pan. Bake at 350° for 35 to 45 minutes or until done. Cool and frost with peach frosting below.

Peach Frosting:
½ cup butter (1 stick), softened to room temperature
1 cup sugar
1 can peach slices (15.25 oz.), drained well and chopped

Beat together butter and sugar. Add peaches and beat together until peaches are "mashed".

Chocolate Applesauce Cake

Yield: 24 servings

1 box Duncan Hines® moist deluxe Dark Chocolate Fudge cake mix (18.25 oz.)
4 eggs
1 jar applesauce (25 oz.)

Pour all ingredients into mixing bowl and beat well. Pour into greased 9 x 13-inch pan and bake at 350° for 45 to 50 minutes. Test for doneness with wooden skewer.

☛ NOTE: *No oil necessary; applesauce takes its place. Very moist and not too sweet. I highly recommend this!*

Kahlúa® Cake

Yield: 24 to 30 servings

1 box yellow cake mix (18.25 oz.)
1 box instant chocolate pudding (3.5 oz.)
4 eggs
1 cup oil
¼ cup Kahlúa®
¾ cup water

Mix all ingredients for 3 minutes. Pour into greased 9 x 13-inch pan. Bake at 350° for 50 minutes or until done.

☛ NOTE: *This cake tastes delicious just as it is. But if you'd like to try the topping, see recipe below.*

Topping:
½ cup powdered sugar
¼ cup Kahlúa®
1 teaspoon instant coffee, powdery texture

Mix ingredients and let sit. While cake is still warm, prick cake before pouring topping over.

Coconut Milk Cake

Yield: 24 to 30 servings

1 box yellow cake mix (18.25 oz.)
1 box instant vanilla pudding mix (3.4 oz.)
½ cup salad oil
4 eggs
½ teaspoon vanilla
1 can frozen coconut milk (12 oz.), thawed

Blend all ingredients (except coconut milk) for 1 minute. Add coconut milk. Beat for another 2 minutes. Pour into greased 9 x 13-inch pan. Bake at 350° for 35 to 40 minutes. Test with skewer for doneness.

☛ NOTE: *Top with frosting of your choice.*

Mango Bread

Yield: 2 loaves

Dry ingredients:

- 2 cups flour
- 2 teaspoons baking soda
- 1 teaspoon cinnamon
- ½ teaspoon salt
- 1¼ cups sugar

Wet ingredients:

- 3 eggs
- ¾ cup oil
- 2 cups mango, diced

Sift together dry ingredients; set aside. In large mixing bowl whisk together eggs and oil. Add dry ingredients and mix until well blended. Fold in diced mango. Pour into 2 greased loaf pans. Bake at 350° for 60 minutes.

☛ NOTE: *Thanks to Berenice Lum who shared this very popular mango bread with us. Her recipe is easy to use and the result is a very tasty and moist mango bread.*

Poppy Seed Bundt Cake

Yield: about 20 servings

- 1 box yellow cake mix (18.25 oz.)
- 1 box instant vanilla pudding (3.5 oz.)
- ½ teaspoon baking powder
- 2 tablespoons poppy seeds
- ¾ cup vegetable oil
- 4 eggs
- 1 cup hot water
- 1 teaspoon almond extract

Mix dry ingredients; add oil. Blend in eggs, one at a time. Add hot water and extract. Bake in greased and floured Bundt pan at 300° for about 50 minutes.

Pineapple Delight

Yield: 12 servings

Crust:

½ cup butter or margarine (1 stick)
1 tablespoon powdered sugar
1 cup flour

Cut ingredients with pastry blender until crumbly. Pat into 9 x 9-inch pan. Bake at 350° for 15 to 20 minutes or until golden brown. Cool.

Filling:

1 package cream cheese (8 oz.)
1 cup milk
1 can crushed pineapple (8 oz.)
1 box instant vanilla pudding (3 oz.)

Blend cream cheese with ¼ cup of the milk. Add rest of milk and pineapple and beat in pudding for 1 minute. Spread mixture over cooled crust. Refrigerate.

☛ NOTE: *Real super easy. Ready to eat soon after because instant pudding sets quickly.*

Pistachio Bundt Cake

Yield: about 20 servings

1 box yellow cake mix (18.25 oz.)
1 box instant pistachio pudding (3.5 oz.)
1 cup 7-Up® soda
1 cup oil
3 eggs
½ cup nuts, chopped (optional)

Mix all ingredients, except nuts, and beat for 2 minutes on medium speed. Mix in nuts, if desired. Pour into greased and floured Bundt pan. Bake at 350° for 45 to 55 minutes.

☛ NOTE: *If using greased and floured 9 x 13-inch pan, bake at 350° for 35 to 45 minutes, or until done.*

Suggestion for frosting if desired:

1 box instant pistachio pudding (3.5 oz.)
2 envelopes Dream Whip®
1½ cups milk

Beat all ingredients until smooth and thick (about 2 to 3 minutes). Spread over cooled cake.

☛ NOTE: *The pistachio cake is delicious by itself! The frosting does make it special, though.*

Quick Banana Bread

Yield: 24 to 30 servings

1 box yellow cake mix (18.25 oz.) (e.g., Duncan Hines® moist deluxe Classic Yellow cake mix)
1 teaspoon baking soda
½ teaspoon baking powder
4 eggs
¾ cup Wesson® oil
1¼ cups bananas, mashed (about 5 to 6 ripe bananas)

Sift dry ingredients; set aside. In another bowl, beat eggs; add oil and mashed bananas. Mix together until well blended. Add in dry ingredients. Pour into greased 9 x 13-inch pan. Bake at 350° for 30 to 35 minutes.

☛ NOTE: *I am very grateful to Joyce Takahashi, a wonderful baker, who generously shared many tasty recipes with me, including this quick banana bread.*

Quick 'n Easy Bread Pudding

Yield: 24 to 30 pieces

½ cup butter (1 stick)
1¼ cups sugar
4 eggs
1 teaspoon vanilla
½ cup raisins
1 pound day old bread, cubed
6 cups milk
Cinnamon, for sprinkling

Beat butter and sugar thoroughly. Add eggs and vanilla; beat well. Add raisins to mixture; mix together. Set aside.

Mix bread and milk together. Add to first mixture; mix thoroughly. Pour into greased 9 x 13-inch pan. Sprinkle top with cinnamon. Bake at 350° for 1 hour. Cut after cooling.

Quick Breakfast Cake

Yield: 9 servings

1 cup flour
½ cup sugar
1 tablespoon baking powder
½ teaspoon cinnamon
2 tablespoons butter, melted
1 egg, beaten
½ cup milk
Cinnamon and sugar, for sprinkling

Sift together dry ingredients. Add egg, milk and butter to dry ingredients. Mix and pour into greased 8 x 8-inch pan. Sprinkle with cinnamon and sugar. Bake at 425° for 20 minutes.

Sizzle Swizzle Cake

Yield: 24 to 30 servings

1 box yellow cake mix (18.25 oz.)
1 box instant pistachio pudding mix (3.5 oz.)
4 eggs, room temperature
¼ cup vegetable oil
½ cup lemon lime soda

Beat together cake mix, pudding, eggs and oil. Add soda and mix again. Pour into greased 9 x 13-inch pan. Bake at 350° for 30 to 35 minutes. Use a skewer to check for doneness.

Quick Red Velvet Cake

Yield: 24 to 30 servings

1 box yellow cake mix (18.25 oz.)
1 teaspoon baking powder
2 tablespoons cocoa
½ cup oil
5 eggs
1 cup buttermilk
1 fl. oz. red food color (¼ cup)

Combine above ingredients and bake according to yellow cake mix cooking instructions. Cool cake and frost.

Cream Cheese Frosting:

1 package cream cheese (8 oz.), softened
¼ cup butter, softened (½ stick butter)
1 cup plus 2 tablespoons powdered sugar
1 teaspoon vanilla extract

Beat together until creamy.

☛ NOTE: *Sift powdered sugar if lumpy.*

Cool Whip® Frosting

Yield: 3 cups

1 package cream cheese (8 oz.), softened to room temperature
1 cup milk
1 container Cool Whip® (8 oz.)
1 box instant pudding, chocolate fudge or any flavor (3 oz.)

Beat cream cheese until smooth and creamy. Add milk slowly, blending well. Add instant pudding and Cool Whip®; mix well. Spread over cake.

Cocoa Buttercream Frosting

Yield: about 2 cups

6 tablespoons butter, softened
2⅓ cups powdered sugar
½ cup Hershey's cocoa
⅓ milk
1 teaspoon vanilla

Beat butter with spoon. Combine powdered sugar and cocoa; add to butter alternately with milk, beating with spoon to spreading consistency. (Add more milk if necessary.) Stir in vanilla.

☛ NOTE: *Very easy to prepare. If needed, powdered sugar and cocoa may be sifted together to remove any lumps. Frosting remains soft and creamy days later.*

White Frosting

Yield: 1 cup

3 oz. cream cheese, softened
¼ cup butter (half stick), softened
1 teaspoon vanilla
2 cups powdered sugar

Beat together cream cheese, butter and vanilla in small bowl until smooth. Gradually add powdered sugar, beating until smooth.

Arare Cookie Crunch

Yield: 5 dozen cookies

¾ cup butter (1½ sticks)
¾ cup margarine (1½ sticks)
1½ cups powdered sugar
2⅔ cups flour
1½ teaspoons vanilla
2 cups crushed arare (Japanese rice crackers)

Beat butter, margarine and sugar. Add flour and vanilla; mix well. Stir in arare. Drop dough by teaspoonfuls onto ungreased baking sheets and flatten slightly. Bake at 325° for 20 minutes or until golden brown.

Almond Cookies

Yield: about 5 dozen

1 cup and 3 tablespoons shortening
1 cup sugar
1 egg, beaten
1 teaspoon almond extract
2½ cups flour
½ teaspoon salt
½ teaspoon baking soda
Red food color

Beat shortening and sugar; add egg and almond extract. Mix well. Sift flour, salt and baking soda; add to sugar and egg mixture. Mix well. Shape into walnut-size balls. Place on ungreased cookie sheet. Using thumb, press center of balls to make a depression. Using the end of a chopstick, dip in red food color and place a dot in the center of each cookie. Bake at 350° for 15 to 18 minutes.

☛ NOTE: *My all-time favorite of all cookies! This recipe is light and crispy!*

Chocolate Cake Cookies

Yield: 36 to 40 cookies

1 box devil's food cake mix (18.25 oz.)
2 eggs, beaten
½ cup vegetable oil
1 cup chopped nuts, raisins or chocolate chips (or any combination)

Mix together all ingredients. Drop a teaspoonful of dough spaced 2 inches apart on ungreased cookie sheet. Bake at 350° for 8 to 10 minutes.

- NOTE: *Very chewy and tasty. I liked it with walnuts and raisins.*

- VARIATION: *Substitute Devil's Food cake mix with other cake mix flavors.*

Granny's Cookies

Yield: 6½ dozen

1¾ cups butter (3½ sticks)
1 cup sugar
1½ teaspoons vanilla
3 cups flour
1¾ teaspoons baking soda
2 cups Rice Krispies®
1 cup Cocoa Krispies®

Beat butter and sugar until creamy. Add vanilla. Sift together flour and baking soda; add to butter mixture in 3 to 4 parts. Fold in Rice and Cocoa Krispies®. Drop by teaspoonfuls on cookie sheet. Bake at 275° for 35 to 40 minutes.

- VARIATION: *Substitute Cocoa Krispies® with package of chocolate chips.*

- NOTE: *Very crispy and light. Everyone's favorite! If rushed, bake at 325° for 15 minutes.*

- NOTE: *Great raves! Very light, crispy and crunchy. A local favorite!*

Shortbread Cookies

Yield: 24 to 30 pieces

1 cup butter or margarine (2 sticks), softened
½ cup sugar
1 teaspoon vanilla
2 cups flour

Beat together butter and sugar until light and fluffy. Add vanilla. Mix in flour. Pat into 9 x 13-inch pan and prick with fork. Bake at 325° for 35 to 40 minutes or until golden in color. Cut into squares while still warm.

Pumpkin Squares

Yield: 40 servings

Crust:
3 cups flour
½ cup sugar
1 cup butter (2 sticks), chilled

Filling:
1 can pumpkin (29 oz.)
2 cans evaporated milk (12 oz. each)
4 eggs, beaten
1½ cups sugar
1 teaspoon cinnamon
1 teaspoon salt

Combine flour and sugar; cut in butter until crumbly. Press into 10 x 16-inch pan. Mix filling ingredients together and spread over crust. Bake at 400° for 15 minutes, then at 350° for 40 minutes.

☛ NOTE: *Crust is a little soft, but the pumpkin filling is very tasty. I liked it!*

Chocolate Drops

Yield: 4 dozen

½ cup butter (1 stick)
3 ounces unsweetened chocolate (6 pieces)
1 cup sugar
1 teaspoon vanilla
¾ cup flour
½ teaspoon baking soda
½ teaspoon salt
2 eggs, beaten

Melt butter and chocolate; cool slightly. Add rest of ingredients; mix well. Drop by teaspoonful onto ungreased cookie sheet. Bake at 375° for 7 to 10 minutes. Place to rack to cool.

☛ NOTE: *So quick and easy! Very similar to "Sponge Drops" in texture. Make it into a special treat by placing a large dollop of mint chocolate chip ice cream between 2 cookies, creating a delicious ice cream sandwich!*

Brownies

Yield: 30 pieces

1 cup butter (2 sticks)
4 squares unsweetened chocolate
3 eggs
2 cups sugar
1 teaspoon vanilla
1 cup flour
½ teaspoon salt
1 cup nuts, chopped (optional)

In small saucepan, melt butter on low heat. Add chocolate; melt and blend together. Set aside to cool. In large bowl, beat eggs with whisk; add sugar and vanilla and stir together. Mix in chocolate mixture. Add flour and salt; blend thoroughly. Add nuts, if desired. Pour into 9 x 13-inch greased pan. Bake at 350° for 45 to 50 minutes. Cut while warm.

Lemon Bars

Yield: 24 to 36 bars

Crust:

1½ cups flour
½ cup powdered sugar
¾ cold margarine or butter (1½ sticks)

Combine flour and powdered sugar; cut in margarine until crumbly. Press onto bottom of lightly greased 9 x 13-inch pan. Bake at 350° for 25 to 30 minutes or until golden brown.

Topping:

4 eggs, slightly beaten
1½ cups sugar
1 teaspoon baking powder
3 tablespoons flour
½ cup lemon juice (about 5 lemons)

While crust is baking, combine topping ingredients and mix well. Pour over baked crust (no need to let crust cool) and return to oven. Bake 20 to 25 minutes or until golden brown. Cool. Cut into bars. Sprinkle with powdered sugar. Store in refrigerator.

☛ NOTE: *This recipe is easier that it looks. Try it. My granddaughters and their cousins love these lemon bars!*

Banana Cream Pie

Yield: 8 servings

1 package cream cheese (8 oz.), softened
3 cups cold milk
2 boxes vanilla instant pudding (3 oz. each)
One 9-inch baked pie crust
(or Keebler's Ready Crust® Shortbread)
2 bananas, sliced
Lite Cool Whip® or other whipped topping

Beat cream cheese until smooth and creamy. Slowly add a little milk, blending together. Continue adding milk and blending. Add instant pudding; mix together until thick. Pour over baked crust lined with sliced bananas. Top with Cool Whip®. Refrigerate.

Custard Pie

Yield: 8 servings

One 9-inch unbaked pie shell
4 eggs
⅔ cup sugar
¼ teaspoon salt
¼ teaspoon nutmeg
½ teaspoon vanilla
2⅔ cups milk, scalded

Beat eggs with fork; combine with sugar, salt, nutmeg and vanilla. Slowly add scalded milk; mix well. Place unbaked pie shell in preheated 425° oven. Then carefully pour custard mixture into unbaked pie shell. Bake at 425° for 25 minutes or until done.

Tofu Pie

Yield: 8 servings

1 Keebler Ready Crust® (graham or butter pie crust)
1 package lemon Jell-O® (3 oz.)
1 cup boiling water
1 to 2 tablespoons lemon juice
½ teaspoon lemon extract
½ of 20 oz. soft tofu
½ container Cool Whip® (half of 8 oz.)

Mix together Jell-O®, boiling water, lemon juice and lemon extract. Refrigerate until slightly firm, about 45 minutes. Drain tofu. Blend tofu and Cool Whip® with electric mixer; mix in Jell-O® mixture. Pour into crust. Refrigerate.

- NOTE: *Delicious! A very smooth and refreshing dessert. I usually double the recipe and make a second tofu pie using strawberry Jell-O®.*

- HINT: *Carefully place pie in refrigerator to chill and set before placing cover over.*

Easy Mint Chocolate Chip Pie

Yield: 8 servings

1 ready made graham cracker pie crust
1 quart mint chocolate chip ice cream
8 oz. Cool Whip®

Soften about 4 cups ice cream (enough to fill pie crust). Spoon into pie crust and freeze. When ready to serve, remove from freezer and leave at room temperature about 10 minutes. Spread Cool Whip® over before slicing.

Key Lime Pie

Yield: 8 servings

1 ready made graham cracker crust (e.g., Keebler Ready Crust®)
Whipped cream or Cool Whip® for topping

Brush egg white on crust and bake for 5 minutes. Set aside to cool.

Filling:

5 yolks of large eggs
1 can Eagle® brand condensed milk
7 tablespoons key lime juice (about 5 to 6 limes)

Whisk together until thoroughly mixed. Pour into cooled crust and bake at 350° for 12 minutes. When pie is cool, spread whipped cream or Cool Whip® over.

☛ SUGGESTION: *Use remaining egg whites in other dishes. For example, make a light omelet by adding another egg, some milk and whatever you have on hand.*

Easy Pie Crust

Yield: One 9-inch pie crust

1½ cups flour
1½ teaspoons sugar
1 teaspoon salt
½ cup oil
2 tablespoons cold milk

Sift together flour, sugar and salt into ungreased 9-inch pie pan. Whip oil and milk with fork until cloudy; pour over flour mixture. Mix with fork until blended. Press dough into pie pan.

☛ NOTE: *For baked pie shell, prick here and there. Bake at 400° for 10 to 15 minutes until light brown.*

Apple Cobbler

Yield: 9 servings

3 large granny smith apples, peeled and sliced
1 cup flour
1 cup sugar
1 teaspoon cinnamon
1 egg
½ cup butter (1 stick), melted

Place apples in lightly greased 8 x 8-inch pan. Mix flour, sugar, cinnamon and egg until it looks like coarse cornmeal. Sprinkle mixture over apples. Pour melted butter over. Bake at 350° for 30 to 35 minutes.

☛ NOTE: *If you love apple desserts, you will love this apple cobbler. Ava Olson did a variation by substituting the 1 cup flour with a combination of ¾ cup flour and ¼ cup Quick Minute® oats which made it healthier. She also tried using apples that she and my nephew, Allan Watanabe, harvested from apple trees growing on the Big Island! Yummy!*

3, 2, 1 Jell-O®

Yield: 16 servings

3 cups boiling water
2 boxes Jell-O® (3 oz. each), any flavor
2 packages Knox® gelatin
1 cup heavy whipping cream

Dissolve Jell-O® and gelatin in boiling water; set aside to cool. Add cream and mix together; pour into 8 x 8-inch pan. Refrigerate until firm.

☛ NOTE: *Kids love this! They'll enjoy helping and seeing what happens when gelatin separates into 2 layers when chilled.*

Energy Bars

Yield: 36 bars

2½ cups Rice Krispies® cereal
1 cup Quick 1 Minute Quaker Oats®
¾ cup roasted sesame seeds
¼ cup butter (½ stick)
½ cup creamy peanut butter
1 package marshmallows (10 oz.)
¼ to ½ cup peanuts
½ cup raisins (or raisin and cranberry combination)

Grease 9 x 13-inch pan; set aside. In frying pan, combine Rice Krispies®, oats and seeds; toast for a few minutes.

In large pot, melt butter over medium-low heat. Add peanut butter and marshmallows; melt and blend over low heat. Stir in cereal mixture, peanuts and raisins. Press in greased pan with greased fingers. Cool. Cut into bars; wrap individually with wax paper or plastic wrap.

☛ NOTE: *Love this! This is one of the easier energy bars to make. Gay Wong of Mutual Publishing really enjoyed this.*

Summer Smoothie

Yield: 2 servings

4 ice cubes, crushed
5 strawberries
1 banana
1 container plain low fat yogurt (8 oz.)
1 cup pineapple juice (or 1 can pineapple juice (6 oz.)), chilled

Crush ice cubes. Add rest of ingredients; blend until smooth. Serve immediately.

Chi Chi Mochi

Yield: 30 pieces

1 box mochiko flour (16 oz.)
2½ cups sugar
1 teaspoon baking powder
1½ to 2 cups water
1 can coconut milk (12 oz.)
1 teaspoon vanilla
Food color, red or green (optional)

Mix dry ingredients in large mixing bowl. Add liquid ingredients and mix thoroughly with whisk. Add few drops food color (if desired). Mix well. Pour into greased 9 x 13-inch pan. Cover tightly with foil. Place in center of oven and bake at 325° for 1 hour. Uncover carefully; cool for several hours or overnight before cutting.

☛ NOTE: *Amount of water affects how soft you prefer the mochi to be.*

Cocoa Mochi

Yield: 30 pieces

2 cups mochiko flour
1¾ cups sugar
1 tablespoon baking soda
3 tablespoons cocoa
2 eggs
1 can evaporated milk (12 oz.)
1 can coconut milk (12 oz.)
¼ cup butter (½ stick), melted
2 teaspoons vanilla

In large bowl, sift together mochiko, sugar, cocoa and baking soda; set aside. In another bowl, lightly beat eggs. Add evaporated milk, coconut milk, butter and vanilla; mix together. Pour into dry ingredients; mix until batter is smooth. Pour into greased 9 x 13-inch pan. Bake at 350° for 1 hour 10 minutes. Cool completely before cutting.

Fresh Blueberry Mochi

Yield: 30 pieces

1 cup butter, melted (2 sticks)
1 $^{2}/_{3}$ cups sugar
1 can evaporated milk (12 oz.)
4 eggs, beaten
1 box mochiko flour (16 oz.)
2 teaspoons baking powder
2 teaspoons vanilla
1 package frozen whole unsweetened blueberries (16 oz.), thawed

Stir sugar in melted butter. Add milk and mix well. Add eggs and mix. Stir in mochiko, baking powder and vanilla. Pour into buttered 9 x 13-inch pan. Fold in blueberries creating a marbleized look. Bake at 350° for 1 hour.

☛ NOTE: *This is my favorite mochi. It brings back memories of my mom who first gave me the original Hilo recipe. It was a big hit whenever I made it.*

Strawberry Goodie-Goodie

Yield: 10 cups

2 cans strawberry soda (Diamond Head® brand preferred)
1 can 7-Up®
1 can condensed milk (Eagle® brand)

Mix together and pour into covered plastic container. Place in freezer. 8 to 9 hours later, mix with fork; place back in freezer. 8 to 9 hours later, mix again.

☛ NOTE: *Kids and adults love strawberry goodie-goodie! After final mixing, goodie-goodie may be transferred to individual cups with lids.*

☛ SUGGESTION: *If desired, use an electric blender on low speed for a smoother texture.*

Jell-O® Mochi

Yield: 90 pieces

1 box mochiko flour (16 oz.)
2 boxes Jell-O®, any flavor (3 oz. each)
1½ cups sugar
2 cans Hawaiian Sun® juice, any flavor (11.5 fl. oz. each)
Potato starch (Katakuriko), for dusting

Combine mochiko, Jell-O® and sugar. Pour juice in center and blend all ingredients thoroughly. Pour into greased and floured 9 x 13-inch pan; cover with foil and seal. Bake at 350° for 1 hour. Remove foil carefully and cool 3 hours or longer. Use plastic knife to cut. Dust with potato starch.

☛ NOTE: *Raynette Kodama, my dental hygienist, who gave me this recipe said her mother often made several Jell-O® flavored mochi to share. So easy to make and so popular with everyone! I tried a combination of lime Jell-O® and Pass-O Guava. Color was a pretty green and it tasted very light and chewy.*

Waffle Treat

Yield: 1 serving

1 waffle, heated
1 scoop vanilla ice cream
Cool Whip® Whipped Topping (7 oz.)
Strawberry syrup (e.g., Hershey's Syrup 22 oz.) or chocolate syrup

Place a scoop ice cream on warm waffle. Squirt Cool Whip® around and over ice cream. Top with strawberry syrup.

☛ NOTE: *I love this! A similar treat was called the "Manager's Special" at the former Kenny's Restaurant in Kaneohe many years ago. It was my favorite dessert then.*

Popo's Pickled Mangoes

Yield: 5 quarts

15 to 20 green mangoes, peeled and sliced
¼ cup Hawaiian salt

Place sliced mangoes in large container. Sprinkle Hawaiian salt over. Let sit for 3 to 5 hours; gently tossing occasionally.

Pickle Sauce:
6 cups water
4 cups sugar
2 cups vinegar

Boil pickle sauce until sugar dissolves; set aside to cool.

Drain and place mangoes in glass jars; pour vinegar mixture over. Refrigerate.

☛ NOTE: *Great pickled mangoes! I received a very similar recipe from Wendy Calizar who adds 1 teaspoon Chinese five spices. Red food color is optional. Another recipe calls for 10 to 20 pieces of Li Hing Mui, if desired.*

Ruby's Easy Furikake Cereal Mix

Yield: 3 quarts

1 box Corn Chex® cereal (14 oz.)
½ cup Nori Komi Furikake

Seasoning:
¼ cup Karo Lite® corn syrup
¼ cup canola oil
3 tablespoons sugar
1 tablespoon soy sauce
5¼ tablespoons butter

Combine seasoning ingredients in a 2-cup Pyrex® glass measuring cup, in the order given. Melt ingredients in microwave oven (about 1 minute). Stir mixture. Set aside.

Pour Chex® cereal into large foil pan sprayed with cooking spray. Drizzle butter mixture over cereal, mixing well until cereal is lightly coated. Sprinkle furikake evenly over cereal; mix well. Bake at 250° for 1 hour, stirring after 30 minutes. Cool. Store in airtight container.

- NOTE: *This is the easiest party mix so far! Ruby says to measure the corn syrup to the ¼ line. Then pour Canola oil up to the ½ line. Add the rest of the seasoning ingredients and microwave.*

- VARIATION: *After cooling, add nuts, pretzel sticks, arare, etc.*

Glossary

'ahi	yellowfin tuna, shibi
aku	skipjack tuna, bonito or katsuo
bitter melon	balsam melon
burrito	tortilla wrapped with filling
Chinese parsley	cilantro
choi sum	Chinese broccoli
chung choi	preserved salted turnip
daikon	white radish or turnip
dashi	soup stock
edamame	soy beans
furikake	rice condiment
furikake nori	seasoned seaweed mix
gobo	burdock root
Hawaiian salt	coarse sea salt
harm ha	shrimp sauce
hoi sin	spicy bean sauce
hondashi	instant Japanese soup stock
inamona	roasted, pounded and salted kukui nut
kamaboko	steamed fish cake
kimchee	hot, spicy preserved vegetable
konnyaku	tuber root flour cake
limu	seaweed
long rice	translucent mung bean noodles
lumpia	spring roll filled with meat, vegetables or fruit
lumpia wrapper	thin flour wrappers for fried rolls
lup cheong	Chinese sweet pork sausage
mazegohan	rice mixed with vegetables and seasoning

mirin	sweet rice wine
miso	fermented soybean paste
mochiko	glutinous rice flour
namako	sea cucumber
ong choy	swamp cabbage
oyster sauce	oyster flavored sauce
panko	flour meal for breading
poke	cut-up pieces of raw fish with seasonings
pupu	appetizer or hors d'oeuvre
sake	rice wine
shiitake	dried mushrooms
soy sauce	soy sauce
somen	fine wheat flour noodles
tabiko	small orange fish eggs
tako	octopus
tempura	fritters
tofu	fresh soybean curd
togan	winter melon squash
tortilla	Mexican flat bread made of cornmeal or wheat flour
wonbok	Chinese cabbage, makina, napa
yatsumi zuke	vegetable relish dish

Index